The Time of Unrememberable Being

... we have learned to speak at the expense of a superior, though certainly deficient language that originally resided within us.

M.A. Goldschmidt *The Heir*, 1865

KLAUS PETER MORTENSEN

The Time of Unrememberable Being

Wordsworth and the Sublime 1787-1805

Translated by W. Glyn Jones

MUSEUM TUSCULANUM PRESS • UNIVERSITY OF COPENHAGEN
1998

The Time of Unrememberable Being

© Klaus Peter Mortensen & Museum Tusculanum Press 1998
Translated from Danish by W. Glyn Jones
Supervisor: Karsten Engelberg
Cover design by Bente Jarlhøj
Text layout by Ole Klitgaard, set in Garamond
Printed in Denmark by AKA PRINT A/S, Aarhus
ISBN 87 7289 443 1

Front and back cover: Two versions of the same prospect of Norham Castle by
J.M.W. Turner from 1798 and c. 1845-50 respectively.
Tate Gallery, London.
(For further comment, see the appendix)

The book has been published with the support of
Dansk litteraturinformationscenter
G.E.C. Gads Fond
Det Humanistiske Fakultet ved Københavns Universitet
Landsdommer V. Gieses legat
Statens Humanistiske Forskningsråd
(The Danish Research Council for the Humanities)

Museum Tusculanum Press
University of Copenhagen
Njalsgade 92
DK-2300 Copenhagen S.

Contents

The Metaphysical Implosion

In his book *Aesthetics and Subjectivity from Kant to Nietzsche*, 1990, Andrew Bowie defines the emergence of modern philosophy as follows: "Modern philosophy begins when the basis upon which the world is interpreted ceases to be a deity whose pattern has already been imprinted into existence and becomes instead our reflection upon our own thinking about the world".[1]

This view is by no means alien to literary historians. For many, Romanticism marks the start of modern literature. Romanticism is closely linked to a comprehensive secularisation of culture which has the subject's self-consideration and self-doubling as one of its essential features. Throughout the literature of the 17th and 18th centuries it is thus possible to follow the way in which the traditional Christian view of life gradually loses its interpretative power, and a new, self-willed subject emerges and seeks to assert its authority.

In the years around 1800, not least German philosophy and literature are seminally concerned with problems of identity raised by this self-willed subject. According to Kant, Man's concept of the world cannot be divorced from the categories of understanding. The subject is thereby imprisoned within its own self or mind, it is no longer possible to speak objectively of the world as such. This profoundly new way of thinking is an important example of what I have chosen to name *the metaphysical implosion*: the widely ramified process in which the sphere reserved for the divine or the numinous in the Christian tradition moves from heaven to earth – first to the great natural phenomena, and then on to the expansive, visionary and creative potential of (divine) human consciousness.

This secularisation and subjectivisation is accompanied by a dizzy sense of freedom, but at the same time it generates a feeling of being exposed, of alienation, of irrepairable loss for the subject who is now to sustain the world and to fill the metaphysical vacuum by his own powers. It is such early ambiguous experiences of joy and fear that are examined in the 18th century under the designation of the Sublime. In the story of how this primarily aesthetical concept was transformed in the course of the 18th century, it is possible to trace the way in which the numinous is transferred from the divine plane attested by nature to the artistic consciousness as revealed in its contemplation and interpretation of nature.

In this revolution the work of William Wordsworth occupies a central, and also unique position. With his poetic examination of the imagination and the Sublime during the period from 1798 and a few years on, Wordsworth blazes the way for a new concept of the relationship between nature and consciousness, and between introspection and retrospection.

This idea, however, should not be considered as an abstract philosophical project, but as a far reaching poetical undertaking. And I shall attempt to examine this undertaking chronologically as far as possible. For during the period c.1798 to 1805, Wordsworth's early writings delve ever deeper into the relationship between nature and consciousness. This poetical process sees the unfolding of a dynamic and visionary form of understanding which was encapsulated in the concept of the Sublime, and which Wordsworth for a time was thus able to deliver in his poetical creation.

Although the ways of presenting the Sublime in philosophy and literature often, not least around 1800, reveal essential points of agreement, it is important to maintain the differences implicit in the genres. Wordsworth's poetry on the Sublime contains aspects which are essentially different from contemporary and later philosophical and aesthetical views on the concept. So if we limit ourselves to define these differences in purely conceptual terms, we will certainly pursue the wrong track. For in Wordsworth's case they are not really dependent on the conceptual as such, but on a different way of thinking which is itself critical of what we normally understand as conceptualisation. Seen through Wordsworth's eyes, conceptualisation limits the power of seeing instead of extending it.

I have allowed myself to be influenced by this attitude in my attempt to understand the language and the form of consciousness that constituted Wordsworth's world of ideas in the crucial years shortly before and after 1800. For the same reason, my readings of Wordsworth's texts are mainly indebted to their artistic strategy, their idiom, and the interrelationship they suggest when – as is the case here – they are seen as elements in an ongoing poetical process.

Quotations have been taken from the following critical editions:

PW: *The Poetical Works of William Wordsworth*, I-V. Edited by E. de Selincourt and Helen Darbishire, Oxford 1967-1972 (1940-1949)

PrW: *The Prose Works of William Wordsworth*, I-III. Edited by W.J.B. Owen and J.W. Smyser, Oxford 1974

N: William Wordsworth *The Prelude* 1799, 1805, 1850. Authoritative Texts, Context and Reception, Recent Critical Essays, Eds. Jonathan Wordsworth, M.H. Abrams, Stephen Gill. A Norton Critical Edition, London 1979

JW: In a few cases quotations are from Jonathan Wordsworth *The Borders of Vision*, Oxford 1982

Where I have thought it useful, references have been given not only to works, volumes and pages but line numbers as well. All translations are, when not otherwise indicated, by W. Glyn Jones.

I would like to express my gratitude to my colleagues Lis Møller and Marie-Louise Svane, to my translator W. Glyn Jones, to Karsten Engelberg, and to the following institutions for the necessary funding of this publication: Dansk litteraturinformationscenter, G. E. C. Gads Fond, Det Humanistiske Fakultet ved Københavns Universitet, Landsdommer V. Gieses legat, Statens Humanistiske Forskningsråd.

Copenhagen, December 1997
Klaus P. Mortensen

CHAPTER 1

Paradise and Paradigm. 1787-1794

The German poet Friedrich Hölderlin described his own poetical stance thus:

> Blissful unity, being in the truest sense of the word, has been lost to us, and we were obliged to lose it if we were to strive for it and to conquer it. We tear ourselves away from the world's peaceful 'hen kai pan' in order to produce it through ourselves. ... It often seems to us as though the world is everything and we nothing, but often also as though we were everything and the world nothing ... To put an end to this eternal conflict between our selves and the world (...) to unite ourselves with nature into one boundless whole, that is the object of our endeavour (...) Nor had we any suspicion of this infinite peace, of this being in the only real meaning of the word – we would not strive to form a union with nature, we would not think and we would not act, (...) unless this boundless union, this being (...) were there nevertheless. It is there in the form of beauty. [2]

Hölderlin depicts a Romantic archetype: The experience of a fundamental loss resulting in a discrepancy between the subject and nature and a corresponding longing to overcome that loss. This is certainly no naive, uncomplicated longing, for it is infused with the consciousness of its own impossibility. For Hölderlin such reflective, illusion-less longing, however, does not lead to resignation, but to an insistence on the beautiful.

Some years before Hölderlin, the nineteen-year-old William Wordsworth treated similar ideas in the short poem *Lines written when sailing in a boat at evening*, 1789:

> How richly glows the water's breast
> Before us, tinged with evening hues,
> While, facing thus the crimson west,
> The boat her silent course pursues!
> And see how dark the backward stream!
> A little moment past so smiling!
> And still, perhaps, with faithless gleam,
> Some other loiterers beguiling.

Such views the youthful Bard allure;
But, heedless of the following gloom,
He deems their colours shall endure
Till peace go with him to the tomb.
– And let him nurse his fond deceit,
And what if he must die in sorrow!
Who would not cherish dreams so sweet,
Though grief and pain may come to-morrow?
(PW I p. 40)

In this poem, Wordsworth touches on one of the fundamental themes in his work: loss and restoration. The experience is portrayed via a clear sequence of steps in the poem's simple composition. In the first stanza the poet is looking ahead towards calm water reflecting the sunset. But this happy sight is eliminated when he turns towards the dark wake of the boat.

The two sense impressions in the first stanza are linked to the surface of the water, and together they suggest a terrestrial horizon. At first the poet's eyes move in a semi-circle from the light in front to the darkness behind, after which the consciousness describes an opposite restorative movement back towards the vanished light, thereby completing the circle. To the qualitative contrast between light and darkness there is a corresponding temporal and spacial one between advancing being in the present moment as the prow cleaves the water, and the regressive reflection concerning the faithless play of colour which is swallowed by the darkness in the stern. Spontaneous surrender to life is replaced by a reflective consciousness of loss or death.

The disappointment arising as the poet's eyes are turned back, however, does not prevent the young man – fully conscious of the darkness awaiting him – from turning back towards the light in the second stanza of the poem recalling the radiant starting point in the belief that it is possible to retain the colours in memory.

This represents a qualitatively different kind of view which while being produced by the immediate sense perception is not tied to it. In this inner vision the young poet, who has divorced himself from the collective "us", believes it will be possible to retain the glowing colours and defy the colourless darkness – until the light of his own consciousness is extinguished in the definitive darkness of death.

12

According to the poem's experienced and sober narrator the young bard is seduced by the brilliance of the sunset rays. But the narrator implies at the same time that there is no alternative to the bard's happy self-deception, to the sweet dreams. Irrespective of whether the bard's dream of colour lasts only for one day or minute or the rest of his life, at least it makes life tolerable until the moment when pain and sorrow and finally death catch up with him.

Although the poem is thus constructed around the basic elements in the traditional Christian view of history that can be summed up in the simple formula: Paradise, Fall, Redemption, it is nevertheless an obviously secular and – as said above – Romantic interpretation. What has been lost cannot without further ado be redeemed. But a reconciliation is effected within the secular framework. In the poet's consciousness, or, more precisely, in its incarnation: the poem, a resurrection takes place in that the poet in memory and imagination returns to his first vision and so keeps the darkness at bay. But this restitution is only a fragile provisional measure created by the poetical ability to form images in the consciousness and language – images that must make up for the loss of the original colours. The poem is an illusion-less illusion. This self-reduplication brings an end to Hölderlins blissful unity.

A correspondingly ambiguous retrospective progression can be found in a still older poetical fragment, the end of an originally longer poem *The Vale of Esthwaite*, 1786-1787. This landscape, too, is seen from a boat,[3] and as in the boat poem the loss and the subsequent retrospective, restorative process are connected with the sinking sun:

> Yet if Heaven bear me far away
> To close the evening of my day,
> If no vast blank impervious cloud
> The powers of thought in darkness shroud,
> Sick, trembling at the world unknown
> And doubting what to call her own,
> Even while my body pants for breath
> And shrinks at the [   ] dart of Death,
> My soul shall cast the wistful view
> The longing look alone on you.
> As Phoebus, when he sinks to rest
> Far on the mountains in the west,
> While all the vale is dark between

Ungilded by his golden sheen,
A lingering lustre softly throws
On the dear hills where first he rose.
(PW I p.281 ll.498-513)

The text forms part of a lengthy description of the Esthwaite Valley. The
fundamental theme is the same as that in the boat poem, the thought of
approaching darkness, death. But while the boat poem starts with the
concrete landscape and finishes with the vision, the order here is reversed.
The poet's starting point is the abstract thought as expressed through the
dead metaphor: the evening of my life. Only at that stage in the text does
the actual valley appear – the valley which his soul will look longingly
back at in death.

In the succeeding literary, almost Homeric development of this progression, the introductory metaphor of the day and night is maintained
and further expanded, and the poem creates an analogy between the
sinking sun throwing its last rays on the countryside and the dying man's
glance. In this analogy between the two farewells, the poet's and the sun's,
the individual human and the cosmic, the personal element in the final
words, "where first he rose" makes the reader think of the speaker, who of
course has come into being in the very hills where the sun rose at the start
of the day. This analogy can be extended to the soul casting his longing
look on the vale and Phoebus' lingering lustre on the dear hills. Just as the
sunlight can be reflected after the sun has disappeared beneath the
horizon, so there is in the soul, in retrospection, the possibility of seeing
what physically has been left behind.

In these lines the young Wordsworth is practising a well-known poetic
strategy in which natural and mental phenomena, the outer and the inner,
reflect each other. But the reflection is at the same time a metaphorical
construction serving to build a bridge between separate and apparently
incompatible spheres. Meanwhile, Wordsworth was not content to form
a verbal analogy. His youthful work can be read as an ever more conscious
endeavour poetically to go beyond the rhetorical strategy he was following
in these early poems and to create a new one. As we shall see, this attempt
rests on the conviction of an earlier, pre-linguistic affinity encompassing
both the physically present natural scenery and human consciousness. In
this poetic process, which extended over several years, Wordsworth
certainly maintained his faith in the reconciling power of the poetical

image, but his conception of this underwent a radical transformation. It is the main steps in this endeavour I shall now attempt to follow.

That Other Eye

Meanwhile, no crucial changes take place in Wordsworth's work in this field until the beginning of 1798. This can be confirmed, for instance, by reading these lines from Wordsworth's 1794 additions to *An Evening Walk*, 1793:

> through the mind, by magic influence
> Rapt into worlds beyond the reign of sense,
> Roll the bright train of never ending dreams
> That pass like rivers tinged with evening gleams.
> (PW I p.9 app. crit.)

The imagery is the same as in the two poems from 1787 and 1789. In the latter, however, the significance of the landscape has changed. Whereas in the 1789 boat poem it is the perceived landscape, the surface of the water that glows in the sunset, here, five years later, it is the inner quality, the dreams, which (in anticipation of Wordswoth's "river of my mind" metaphor in *The Prelude*) is seen as flowing rivers coloured by the sinking sun. But the actual analogisation of the natural phenomenon and the process of consciousness is fundamentally the same here in 1794 as in 1787. Wordsworth is still using nature metaphorically.

The same applies to another passage which Wordsworth added in 1794 to *An Evening Walk*. In it he describes "those favoured souls" who can see a deeper meaning in natural phenomena than that which sense perception immediately offers.

> Blest are those spirits tremblingly awake,
> Yes, thou art blest, my friend, with mind awake
> To Nature's impulse like this living lake,
> Whose mirror makes the landscape's charms its own
> With touches soft as those to Memory known;
> While exquisite of sense the mighty mass
> All vibrates to the lightest gales that pass.
> (PW I p.12 app.crit.)

This extreme sensitivity in relation to nature, which is that of his friend – his sister Dorothy[4] – is illustrated by means of a nature metaphor in which, as in the 1787 fragment, the natural phenomena point beyond themselves and become images of human consciousness. The trembling wakeful spirit is just as receptive as the soul-less water in the lake which reacts to the slightest breeze and welcomes the beauties of the landscape in its reflecting, ever-moving surface with "touches soft as those to Memory known".

But within this framework something new is emerging in the form of a deeper understanding, the inner process hidden beneath the "as" of the comparison. And this understanding of the process of forming a poetical image is in itself linked to the very metaphorical language Wordsworth is creating, especially his use of the phenomenon of reflection which determines the overall structure of the poem – and the creative poetical mind. For in the course of the metaphorical comparison of the lake's receptive surface and the human mind the image moves from a literally superficial similarity: reflection as passive mirroring, to a dissimilarity: the reflection as the receiver's active, (trans)forming reproduction of what is received. So the image of the mind *as* a vibrating and reflecting surface of water also contains an image of an image, or more precisely: an image of the creation of an image that differs from nature's purely unconscious ("exquisite of sense"), passive reflection of the landscape or the wind. For the mind is not tied either physically or temporally to its surroundings as is the surface of the water, which is there simply as an inarticulate, physical mass. The human reflection of nature encompasses memory and is thereby an active creative process adding gentle (brush) strokes – as "touches soft" can also mean – to the landscape in exactly the same way as an artist does when recalling, re-creating nature with colours on a canvas or with words on paper. Wordsworth thus describes the imagination as at once receptive and creative. This change in the function of the reflected image in Wordsworth corresponds to the development which the mirror metaphor undergoes in the course of the 18th century, when from being an imperfect reproduction – as it is in the idea of nature as a mirror in which Man can sense the Creator – the mirror becomes a symbol of the complex relationship between the sensing, understanding and creating self and the world.

This twofold reflection is characteristic of the "favoured souls" as distinct from ordinary people who are blind to the grandeur of nature:

> How different with those favoured souls who, taught
> By active Fancy or by patient Thought,
> See common forms prolong the endless chain
> Of joy and grief, of pleasure and of pain;
> But chiefly those to whom the harmonious doors
> Of science have unbarred celestial stores,
> To whom a burning energy has given
> That other eye which darts thro' earth and heaven,
> Roams through all space and [ ] unconfined,
> Explores the illimitable tracts of mind,
> And piercing the profound of time can see
> Whatever man has been and man can be.
> (PW I pp.12-13 app.crit.)

By active imagination and patient thought, these titans are able to transcend the senses' links to time and space, to explore the unbounded landscapes of the mind and to recognise human nature beyond time.

This transcendental drive towards the unity of all things is also felt in another passage added in 1794. Here we again find the vibrating, receptive surface of the water as the seat of the feelings: the receptive heart whose ability to expand is without limit and leads to the elimination of all boundaries. Life, being, is infinite in time and space.

> A heart that vibrates evermore, awake
> To feeling for all forms that Life can take,
> That wider still its sympathy extends
> And sees not any line where being ends ...
> (PW I p.10 app.crit.)

The Sublime Track

In this programmatic, metaphorical movement from the landscape without to the regions within, from the limited to the limitless and thereby to an experience of unity, the contours are drawn of what I will call the sublime track in Wordsworth's poetry: The idea that in his meeting with great nature – in this case the masses of water – Man can experience a corresponding greatness in himself ("illimitable tracts of mind"). The organ of this greatness is the seeing heart or "that other eye": the ability of consciousness to transcend normal boundaries of sensing and understanding, an ability born of the formative receptiveness towards nature which the young Wordsworth sought to pin down in the image of the trembling surface of the lake with its gentle strokes, and of the vibrating and illimitable heart.

With its description of the relationship between the great nature without and a great nature within, between objective and subjective, the poem at the same time raises the question as to the kind of sublimity revealing itself here. Is it a relationship in which man – through an identity between the physical nature of the landscape and man's spiritual nature – can move cognitially from the outer to the inner? Or is it a question of staging the self's ability to understand, projecting nature within on nature without, of diverting attention from the elementary but also transitory world of the body?

If we limit ourselves to the poems from 1787 and 1789 and the additions to *An Evening Walk* from 1794, the answer seems to be quite simple: it is a case of the latter – an attempt at removing the distinction between consciousness and nature through the use of metaphors, an attempt which moreover has become noticeably intensified between 1789 and 1794. From illusion-less illusion to pure and simple willed illusion making. In the boat poem loss and darkness are associated with man's ties to nature and the poet can defy them only for a short time and in sweet illusion. In contrast to this the fragment attempts partly to ignore the loss, partly to relate man and nature in an analogy. But the analogy cannot be maintained; on the contrary, it underlines the loss and the separation, for it rests on an express distinction between the very two entities it ought to unite: unarticulated, pure being in nature and conscious human existence.

Nevertheless, it is possible – as I will attempt to argue in the following – to trace a determined and intense effort in Wordsworth's work to maintain the relationship between consciousness and nature as something other than a projection, that is to say as depending on a more fundamental equality than metaphorical likeness. This attempt culminated in 1798 and 1799, when Wordsworth formed his own deeply personal view of the relationship between nature and consciousness. Not in a theoretical and programmatic, but a poetical form by way of a profounder understanding of the power and nature of the imagination and an original interpretation of the key aesthetical concept of the time: the Sublime.

If we want to have a sense of the true dimensions of this poetical and cognitive breakthrough, we must see it against the background of the complex of ideas covered by the idea of the Sublime in Wordsworth's day.

CHAPTER 2

The Nature of the Sublime – A Historical Sketch

> Die Natur ist dem Künstler nicht mehr als sie
> dem Philosophen ist, nämlich nur die unter be-
> ständigen Abschränkungen erscheinende ideali-
> sche Welt, oder nur der unvollkommene Wie-
> derschein einer Welt, die nicht ausser ihm, son-
> dern in ihm existirt.
> Fr. Schelling: *System des transcendentalen Idealismus*,
> 1800[5]

The Ugly and the Beautiful

In his first autobiographical sketch, *Levnedsbrev,* from 1728, the Danish author and professor Ludvig Holberg describes his journey to the South 1714-16. The following comment is taken from the account of his journey home from Rome in 1716: "From Turin I travelled over the Alpine Mountains and came to Savoy, which country, though filled with rocks and ugly to behold, nevertheless contains many beautiful towns and cities".[6]

The mountains are troublesome, ugly piles of rocks that create difficulties for the young traveller – but on the other hand the beautiful towns reward his pains. When the English author Thomas Gray wrote home to his mother in 1739 and told her of his experience of the Alps, the tone was notably different:

> It is six miles to the top; the road runs winding up it, commonly not six feet broad; on one hand is the rock, with woods of pine-trees hanging overhead; on the other a monstrous precipice, almost perpendicular, at the bottom of which rolls a torrent, that sometimes tumbling among the fragments of stone that have fallen from on high, and sometimes precipitating itself down vast descents with a noise like thunder, which is still made greater by the echo from the mountains on each side, concurs to form one of the most solemn, the most romantic, and the most astonishing scenes I ever beheld: add to this the strange views made by the crags and cliffs on the other hand; the cascades that in many places throw themselves from the very summit down into the vale, and the river below; and many other particulars impossible to describe; you will conclude we had no occasion to repent our pains.[7]

The mountain scenery here is wild, violent and impassable, but also entrancing and romantic – it produces a solemn mood in Gray. In this dual quality of wild, threatening natural scenery and spiritual elevation a new concept of nature and humanity is in the making.

The fact that Holberg and Gray feel aversion and attraction respectively when faced with mountain scenery, the uncivilised, "wild" and grand natural scenery, is not merely the result of the difference in temperament. The two statements can also be read as signs of the profound change taking place in the view of nature in the 18th century throughout Europe, not least in England. Holberg's inability to tolerate the piles of rocks is paradoxically not the result of his being more of a modern town dweller than Gray, but rather the contrary. Urbanisation and the establishment of bourgeois society had gone much further in Gray's native land than in Holberg's.

So the change in the view of nature can be seen in relation to the emergence and establishment of bourgeois culture and thus bourgeois individualism in the 18th century – a process taking place at different times from country to country, but with England in the lead. Put simply: as people move into the towns, leaving behind the countryside and their immediate contact with and dependence on nature, this has consequences for their views on nature and the individual. This can be felt in the following passage from Goethe's Faust, 1808, describing how the town dweller experiences the coming of spring:

Aus dem hohlen, finstern Tor
Dringt ein buntes Gewimmel hervor.
Jeder sonnt sich heute so gern
Sie feiern die Auferstehung des Herrn;
Denn sie sind selber auferstanden:
Aus niedriger Häuser dumpfen Gemächern,
Aus Handwerks- und Gewerbes-Banden,
Aus dem Druck von Giebeln und Dächern,
Aus der Straßen quetschender Enge,
Aus der Kirchen ehrwürdiger Nacht
Sind sie alle ans Licht gebracht.
Sieh nur, sieh! Wie behend sich die Menge
Durch die Gärten und Felder zerschlägt,
Wie der Fluß in Breit und Länge
So manchen lustigen Nachen bewegt;

Und bis zum Sinken überladen,
Entfernt sich dieser letzte Kahn.
Selbst von des Berges fernen Pfaden
Blinken uns farbige Kleider an.
Ich höre schon des Dorfs Getümmel;
Hier ist des Volkes wahrer Himmel,
Zufrieden jauchzet Groß und Klein:
Hier bin ich Mensch, hier darf ich's sein.[8]

Liberation from urban civilisation has both physical and metaphysical dimensions: To Goethe, Christ's resurrection is a symbol of man's rising to his forgotten or suppressed true human dignity, which is to be found away from the city, the workplace and the church – out in the midst of nature. Thus man finds his own originality, his true nature, his natural-ness, beyond the conventional boundaries for true humanity set by civilisation. Wordsworth's *The Prelude*, 1805, is introduced in a similar way with an image of liberation from the town and a return to the true humanity of nature:

Oh there is blessing in this gentle breeze,
That blows from the green fields and from the clouds
And from the sky; it beats against my cheek,
And seems half conscious of the joy it gives.
O welcome messenger! O welcome friend!
A captive greets thee, coming from a house
Of bondage, from yon city's walls set free,
A prison where he hath been long immured.
Now I am free, enfranchised and at large,
May fix my habitation where I will.
...
I breathe again -
Trances of thought and mountings of the mind
Come fast upon me. It is shaken off,
That burthen of my own unnatural self.
(N p.28 ll.1-10 and 19-23)

The movement out into nature is a liberation from un-nature, for urban culture is an alienation from real, true human nature. Therefore the movement out into nature is at the same time a restorative movement back towards a lost original state.

In this simple pattern of thought we find one of the fundamental notions of bourgeois culture: the secularised idea of the lost paradise as a paradise in nature which can be visited and found outside the boundaries of civilisation, but nevertheless within those set by time and space. We shall shortly confront this idea again in Addison, but first we are to encounter it in Wordsworth's own words in *Prospectus to The Excursion,* written in January 1800, and here quoted in the form it received in the 1814 edition:

> Paradise, and Groves
> Elysian, Fortunate Fields – like those of old
> Sought in the Atlantic Main – why should they be
> A history only of departed things,
> Or a mere fiction of what never was?
> For the discerning intellect of Man,
> When wedded to this goodly universe
> In love and holy passion, shall find these
> A simple produce of the common day.
> (PrW III p.7 ll.105-113)

According to this way of thinking, then, paradise is not to be found in heaven, but here on earth. Man, if he dares and has the strength to do so, can battle his own way to paradise, original nature – outside civilisation or the city – where everything is as it should be and always was. In nature – both outer and inner – man has access to the divine, and his true original self: "Hier bin ich Mensch".

The Book of Nature
On the face of it, Wordsworth's removing paradise out into nature constitutes a breach with the traditional Christian view of nature. But at the same time the breach is in line with a well-established Christian concept with roots stretching right back to St Paul.[9] Christian theology draws a sharp distinction between two kinds of nature: the sinful and transitory earthly nature and the divine supra-nature, but the distinction does not imply that the two are unrelated. This way of thinking has played an important role over the years, not least in the 17th century, and it presents nature as a book which man can read in the same way as he reads the Bible and find in it evidence of God's power, goodness and wisdom. In the words of Johannes Kepler from 1618:

For the world is the very Book of Nature in which God as Creator has revealed and depicted His being and His will with Man in a wordless tract.[10]

However, nature is not only conceived of as a book, but also as "a beautiful image/ figure and painting"[11] or as a mirror. Edward Young put it this way in *Night Thoughts*, 1742-1744:

> *Nature* is the glass reflecting God,
> As, by the *sea*, reflected is the *Sun*.[12]

The illustration to the 1734 edition of Johann Arndt's *Vier Bücher vom wahren Christenthum*, which first appeared in 1614, is based on the very same fundamental idea (see the illustration p. 26). A common feature in all metaphors relating to the book of nature is that the phenomena of nature and the cyclical pattern of nature are considered as a sign pointing back towards a will that cannot itself be sensed or comprehended. As Johann Arndt puts it in *Liber naturae; eller Natvrspeyel*, (i.e.: Mirror of Nature) 1618: "What is the beauty of heaven and the whole of creation other/ (...) than a mirror/ in which shines the supreme Creator's masterpiece?"[13] However, it is possible to trace or to sense God in His work. "For GOD has built into all creatures a sign or footmark/ by which he can trace the Creator." Thus the mirror metaphor implies that the image is indirect as the elaborate frontispiece to O.Traber's *Nervus Opticus*, 1675 suggests[14] (see the illustration p. 27). The light of God, himself unseen, is reflected by the sun, the sun in turn being reflected by way of a heavenly, spiritual mirror (contrasting the speculum to the right reflecting physical light) reflecting and revealing the name of Christ illuminating or heading a mirror signifying the Holy Scriptures. The zig-zag course of this communication is at the same time an interpretation of the words of St. Paul in his First Epistle to the Corinthians Ch. 13,12: "For now we see through a glass, darkly; but then face to face" - on the illustration alluded to by the words: "Nunc Per Speculum".

Man may not and cannot see God. It is this - apparently sometimes very complicated - idea of the mirror and its metaphysical consequences that Wordsworth transforms in his early work and subsequently expands making it a fundamental feature of his nature dialectic in 1798-1800.

Illustration to the 1734 edition of Johann Arndt, *Vier Bücher vom wahren Christentum.*

Frontispiece from O. Traber, *Nervus Opticus*, 1675.

17th century interest in nature as an indication of the Creator is turned in a distinctly new direction at the end of the century. This can, for instance, be observed in the first volume of Thomas Burnet's *The Sacred Theory of the Earth* from 1681. He characterizes the great natural phenomena, the firmament, the oceans and the mountains in this way:

> There is something august and stately in the Air of these things, that inspires the Mind with great Thoughts and Passions; we do naturally, upon such Occasions, think of God and his Greatness: And whatsoever hath but the Shadow and Appearance of INFINITE, as all Things have that are too big for our Comprehension, they fill and over-bear the Mind with the Excess, and cast it into a pleasing kind of Stupor and Admiration.
> And yet these Mountains (...) are nothing but great Ruins; but such as shew a certain Magnificence in Nature.[15]

As a result of the Flood the Earth in its present state is to Burnet a ruin compared with its original, perfect form. Although the ruin is thus testimony to the sinfulness of earthly nature, it is nevertheless primarily a sign that a revolution has taken place in nature, presupposing the powerful intervention of God. In this way the great mountains are also a token of God's omnipotence. Indeed, even the great fundamental rhythms of nature, in which everything is subject to violent transformation, are a prefiguration of a higher, supra-natural order and its great author:

> There would be nothing great or considerable in this inferior world, if there were not such revolutions of nature. The seasons of the year, and the fresh productions of the spring, are pretty in their way; but when the Great Year comes about, with a new order of all things, in the heavens and on the earth; and a new dress of nature throughout all her regions, far more goodly and beautiful than the fairest spring; this gives a new life to the creation, and shows the greatness of its author.[16]

The idea of the Book of Nature is thus still present in Burnet's theological-geological speculations. But Burnet's presentation of nature is at the same time an early example of what in the 18th century was thoroughly explored within Longinus' idea of the Sublime: The mighty elevation of the mind when confronted by the incomprehensibly great in nature. Burnet's words can therefore also be read as evidence that when we meet the concept of the Sublime in the aesthetics of the 18th century, it might very well be inspired by the reception of Longinus, but as Marjorie Hope Nicholson rightly points out in *Mountain Gloom and Mountain Glory*, 1959, the attitudes constituting the very substance of the Sublime existed before the reintroduction of the concept itself:

> The sense of the 'Sublime' in external Nature (...) was not, as it has usually been interpreted, the result of a literary tradition stemming from the rediscovery of Longinus. The Sublime had come to England well before the rhetorical theories of Longinus began to interest Englishmen. Awe, compounded of mingled terror and exultation, once reserved for God, passed over in the seventeenth century first to an expanded cosmos, then from macrocosm to the greatest object in the geocosm – mountains, ocean, desert.[17]

This transfer of the divine to nature can be observed in the way in which sublime experiences are conceptualised on the basis of already existing Christian metaphysics of nature. The fundamental idea that the greatness of the Creator can be derived from His works allows a new, secular view of nature to emerge gradually within the Christian realm of ideas without being seen as heresy.

Thus the transfer of divinity to nature could take place so painlessly because the basic concepts of the divinity and the corresponding religious needs were maintained in the concept of the Sublime. In 1917 Rudolph Otto published his phenomenology of religious experience in *Das Heilige*.[18] His self-invented key concept, the numinous, consists of two components: Man feels totally annihilated when faced by the frightening majesty of the numinous:

> Sie führt zu der 'annihilatio' des Selbst auf der einen Seite und zu der Allein- und All-realität des Transzendenten auf der anderen Seite (...).[19]

But at the same time the numinous is also fascinating, compelling:

> Das qualitative Gehalt des Numinosen (an den das Mysteriosum die Form gibt), ist einerseits das schon ausgeführte abdrängende Moment des tremendum mit der 'majestas'. Anderseits aber ist er offenbar zugleich etwas eigentümlich Anziehendes, Bestrickendes, Faszinierendes, das nun mit dem abdrängenden Momente des tremendum in eine seltsame Kontrast-Harmonie tritt.[20]

Now, precisely this violent tension between opposite extremes: annihilation and elevation, fear and delight, is transferred by the new secular ideas of nature from the experience of the divinity to the individual experience of nature which we have already observed in Gray's letter. Preoccupation with the Sublime is thus a significant element in the process of secularisation. Put very briefly: In the process which I have called the metaphysical implosion, the elevated is moved from the confessional, religious, institutional sphere to an aesthetic(-religious) sphere, from church to nature, which in turn becomes a sacred place. But this sacred nature is expressly incapsulated in the aesthetic. Thus during the 18th century art clearly acquires metaphysical functions, not as the servant of an institution, but in its own right and in its own name. It is not least in this connection that the aesthetic concept of the Sublime and of sublime nature acquire their role as important vehicles for the transition to a new idea of nature.

In this way the traditional view of nature as a picture God has painted so that man can have a sense of His omnipotence appears to survive in the new secularised view of nature, for instance with Wordsworth in this fragment from 1798:

> ... The eternal spirit – he that has
> His life in unimaginable things,
> And he who painting what he is in all
> The visible imagery of all the worlds
> Is yet apparent chiefly as the soul
> Of our first sympathies.
> (N p.489 ll.104-109)

To Wordsworth the eternal spirit is still the painter revealing his incomprehensible being in the metaphorical language of nature. However, although the key metaphors in the old language are preserved in the letter their impact has changed dramatically. Having reflected the extra-human, divine nature now comes imperceptibly to reflect the intra-human. God is no longer the supreme Creator God, raised high above the work of creation, for he is woven together with man's elementary emotional nature and its genesis. The new meaning, then, does not emerge as a breach, a sudden change of paradigm, but evolves within the traditional way of thinking.

Nature as Landscape

The longing for and worship of grand, often wild, dangerous nature evolving in the 17th and 18th centuries must be understood in this context. We have already been presented with a characteristic selection of natural phenomena linked to this worship of sublime nature in Burnet: the (starry) heavens, the ocean, the mountains.

These and other phenomena assume an almost emblematic character – as is confirmed by the landscape painting and poetry of the 17th and 18th centuries with their recurrent motifs: panoramic, cosmic-dramatic stretches of landscape displaying the might of natural forces and man's insignificance as he battles with them.

The growing aesthetic interest in nature implies that nature assumes the form of a definable object, a fragment which nevertheless at the same time makes a cosmic claim. Nature becomes a *landscape*, a fashioned whole – individual and universal at the same time. On the one hand many of the landscape paintings and poems represent specific localities, on the other the individual landscape is a manifestation of the supra-individual. This is one of the reasons why the grand nature of the 18th century can act a mirror both to a universal metaphysical order and to the individual's divine potential.

Those who formulate the new concept of landscape are however not themselves part of what they are describing and fashioning. Only at an aesthetic distance does it become possible to determine and compose the fragment of cosmic nature which the landscape represents. In a cultural sense, the composing mind belongs to a person whose social reality is separated from life and work in nature. "The aesthetic view of nature has arisen in the cities simply because an aesthetic view demands distance, alienation".[21] The town dweller has freed himself from the compulsion imposed by nature. Nature is no longer an indissoluble part of his existence, it is not the basis for his life, and although he may still to a certain extent be subject to its climatic whims, his life is not immediately dependent on it.

We have met a trace of this new attitude in Gray, and we can certainly find it in the visual art and literature of the period – and in a very tangible way in English landscape gardening to which at the beginning of the 18th century were ascribed new ideals as it moved in the direction of the "natural", i.e. not (visibly!) arranged, garden. In her book *Landscape*

and Ideology Ann Bermingham demonstrates how the concept of natural-
ness established itself as the vehicle of an ideology at the same time as the
enclosure and cultivation of the extensive areas of generally accessible
common land in the English landscape was taking place. "As the real
landscape began to look ever more artificial, the garden began to look ever
more natural, like the landscape before it was enclosed".[22]

This process lasts a good hundred years from 1740. According to
Bermingham, the property assumed two distinct functions: cultivated
nature, the fields and meadows became a symbol of the owner's social
status. This was previously demonstrated by the garden, while the garden
now conversely came to represent uncultivated – free, unbound, true –
nature. Bermingham's point of view might thus be extended to incorporate the view that the natural garden also had a social function as a sign
of the owner's station as the absolute master of nature including human
nature. From such a point of view the natural garden betokened the
naturalisation of power and control which were replacing the ancient
aristocracy's power by divine right and the old forms of direct manifestation of power displayed, for instance, in the geometrical patterns of the
socalled "French" garden. But it was not only a matter of physical garden
plans. The new landscape gardening implied a quite new conception of
authority and human identity.

One of the most prominent spokesmen for the new landscape
gardening – and also the first modern theoretician of the Sublime – was
Joseph Addison, who wrote about his own garden in *The Spectator* for 6
September 1712. His words can at the same time be read as evidence of
how this idea of naturalness looked at an early stage of its historical
development:

> I have several acres about my House, which I call my garden, and which a
> skilful Gardener would not know what to call. It is a confusion of Kitchin and
> Parterre, Orchard and Flower Garden, which lie so mixt and interwoven with
> one another, that if a foreigner, who had seen nothing of our country, should
> be conveyed into my Garden at his first landing, he would look upon it as a
> natural wilderness, and one of the uncultivated Parts of our country. My
> flowers grow up in several Parts of the Garden in the greatest Luxuriancy and
> Profusion. (...) There is the same irregularity in my Plantations, which run into
> as great a Wildness as their natures will permit. I take in none that do not
> naturally rejoice in the Soil, and am pleased when I am walking in a Labyrinth
> of my own raising, not to know whether the next Tree I shall meet with is an

32

Apple or an Oak, an Elm or a Pear-tree. (...) I must not omit, that there is a Fountain rising in the upper Part of my Garden, which forms a little wandering Rill, and administers to the Pleasure as well as the Plenty of the Place. I have so conducted it, that it visits most of my Plantations, and have taken particular Care to let it run in the same manner as it would do in an open Field. (...) As my Garden invites into it all the Birds of the Country, by offering them the Conveniency of Springs and Shades, Solitude and Shelter, I do not suffer any one to destroy their nests in the spring, or drive them from their usual Haunts in Fruit time. I value my Garden for being full of Black-birds and Cherries, and very frankly give them Fruit for their Songs. By this means I have always the Musick of the Season in its Perfection (...)

You must know, sir, that I look upon the Pleasure which we take in a Garden, as one of the most innocent Delights in Human Life. A Garden was the Habitation of our first Parents before the Fall. It is naturally apt to fill the Mind with Calmness and Tranquillity, and to lay all its turbulent Passions at rest. It gives us a great Insight into the Contrivance and Wisdom of Providence, and suggests innumerable Subjects for Meditation.[23]

Addison's garden is a carefully arranged wilderness – a nature paradise emotionally linking us to our original being before the Fall. Once put in place, the plants are allowed to grow freely, but constantly watched and regulated by a highly conscious owner who loves to observe his work of creation. So, when Addison delights in walking about in his irregular "natural" labyrinth, following the "natural" meanderings of the carefully controlled brook and enjoying the "natural" music of the birds, this is closely related to the fact that he senses nature not only as a simple physical entity, but as true, original nature, the antithesis of the other, "unnatural", highly stylised nature of the aristocrats. At the same time, however, this nature is not unpredictable and uncontrollable as a real wilderness can be. Everything is under control, nature is peaceful, and Addison can be completely unconcerned about whether the thrushes eat his cherries, for he is not going to live by selling them or to eat them himself. So art and artificiality is still there; Addison has merely camouflaged it as nature. Birds do not go in for music, flowers do not create paintings, and human beings cannot produce a wilderness. Nevertheless, for Addison they still do. Stubbornly and determinedly.

The praises he sings of his work of creation can therefore be read as an indirect portrayal of how the bourgeois view of itself is objectified as pure and unspoilt nature – in carefully but surreptitiously controlled untamed nature. Addison thus anticipates all the contradictory ideology of naturalness that was to become the foundation of bourgeois self-understanding, in which nature is no longer the mirror in which we can vaguely distinguish God, but the mirror in which we see ourselves and nothing but ourselves.

This interpretation receives a concentrated philosophical formulation in the introductory quotation to the present chapter from Schelling. Nature – the sun – is basically still a reflection of the divine and nature still a mirror of a spiritual reality. To both the philosopher and the poet nature is the emergence of an ideal world or the imperfect reflection – "Wiederschein" – of a world existing not outside but within the poet himself. Thus the source of the reflection has changed dramatically.

In the same way, but in a far more subdued, down-to-earth form, the nature garden acts as self-confirmation for Addison. In the labyrinthine paradise garden, man returns to the original state he lost in the Fall. Addison's garden – unspoiled nature – is the concrete, physical place in which man can leave behind him the confusion of passions and step into a meditative peace that enables him to gain an insight into the ways of providence, that is to say into the fundamental laws governing life. Thus the garden has social, psychological and metaphysical dimensions at one and the same time. It is not in society, but in unspoiled nature that man discovers his true nature. The withdrawal into and contemplation of nature is thus a kind of ideal model for the reflection and self-reflection on which bourgeois individualism is based. It is the natural way to be a human being. Naturally.

But the entire complex of creating a natural, peaceful impression, and yet maintaining a distance to nature could also be interpreted as the expression of wishful thinking in which man dreams of being free from necessity, from all those aspects of nature that cannot be controlled – ultimately the death that is part of all biological life. In the aesthetic (or technological) establishment of distance from nature, there is therefore also an inherent fear. And this fear cannot be overcome, though it might be possible to displace it for instance in the aesthetic interpretation of man's conditions within and without, as happens with Addison. In this complicated way fear of nature and sentimentality towards nature – or the longing for a natural paradise – are interwoven in the fundamentally impossible, paradoxical aim of the new aesthetics: to go back on themselves by making art natural, ie. neutralising the fall caused by aesthetic (and technological) separation from nature. On this point, the concept of the Sublime with its abundance of contradictions – first and foremost the conflicting feelings of pain and pleasure – offered itself as an answer to the need created by culture for an overall aesthetic interpretation of human life and nature providing rhetorical or symbolical control of the violent conflicting powers to which man is subjected by being a self-reflective creature.

The Nature of the Sublime

Christian C.L. Hirschfeld's *Theorie der Gartenkunst*, 1779-1780, is a splendid example of how this answer was framed in the last part of the 18th century, and how, as part of this process, the numinous was transferred to nature in the form of (sublime) landscape, whence it extends to man – in the landscape. The new correspondence between (divine) nature and consciousness is unfolded in the book's description of the bourgeois metaphysics of the landscape. The landscape is the setting for a spiritual urge to expand – with social and perhaps in this case also political overtones – very much like what we have met in embryonic form in Addison and later in Goethe and Wordsworth. Hirschfeld's reflections are an impressive demonstration, partly of how physical and psychological nature are brought together in a dialectic interplay, partly of the fundamentals offered by the theories of the age concerning the Sublime:

> Wir hassen Einschränkung und lieben Ausdehnung und Freiheit (...) Das Anschauen kleiner Vorwürfe auf einem abgezirkelten Platz, wie bald sättigt es nicht und erregt Ekel! Wie erquickend ist dagegen der Anblick einer ganzen Landschaft, Berge, Felsen, breiten Gewässern, Waldungen! Wie sehr erweitert sich nicht die ganze Seele, spannet alle ihre Kräfte an, arbeitet, um alles zu erfassen, wenn sich die Aussicht auf den Ozean voraus eröffnet, oder wenn in einer hellen Winternacht die gränzenlose Schöpfung voll leuchtender Planeten und brennender Fixsterne sich unserm Auge zu entwickeln scheint! Die Liebe des Menschen zum Grossen, die seine höhere Bestimmung anzukündigen scheint, wirkt so stark und sichtbar, dass an ihrer Wahrheit nicht mehr gezweifelt werden kann (...) Man erhebt sich von dem gewöhnlichen niedrigen Standort hinauf zu einer Sphäre der Bilder und der Empfindung. Man fühlt es, dass man nicht mehr der alltägliche Mensch, sondern ein Wesen von einer Kraft und Bestimmung ist, die weit über den Punkt, auf welchen wir stehen, hinausragt.[24]

Man is reflected in grand nature and sees the potential of his own being in it. In contrast to what is narrow and limiting, there is the boundless, grand landscape, and this contrast in the world of phenomena corresponds to man's sense of respectively a lack of freedom and freedom. The shift from the former to the latter sees an expansion in the form of an inner elevation. Thus the sublime experience becomes internalised, physical grandeur transformed into spiritual grandeur – while correspondingly the world of phenomena becomes a symbol of inner, human realities.

In the spring of 1804[25], when he created his intense poem on landscape and mountains, *The Simplon Pass*, William Wordsworth was thus writing within an already well-established frame of thinking. The poem can actually be read as a paradigm of the concept of the Sublime as featured in the nature poetry of that time as well as in visual art, like Turner's contemporary *The Passage of the St. Gothard*, c. 1804.

> ———— Brook and road
> Were fellow-travellers in this gloomy Pass,
> And with them did we journey several hours
> At a slow step. The immeasurable height
> Of woods decaying, never to be decayed,
> The stationary blasts of waterfalls,
> And in the narrow rent, at every turn,
> Winds thwarting winds bewildered and forlorn,
> The torrents shooting from the clear blue sky,
> The rocks that muttered close upon our ears,
> Black drizzling crags that spake by the wayside
> As if a voice were in them, the sick sight
> And giddy prospect of the raving stream,
> The unfettered clouds and regions of the heavens,
> Tumult and peace, the darkness and the light –
> Were all like workings of one great mind, the features
> Of the same face, blossoms upon one tree,
> Characters of the great Apocalypse,
> The types and symbols of Eternity,
> Of first, and last, and midst, and without end.
> (PW II p. 212-213)

Both Gray and Hirschfeld would have nodded in recognition of Wordsworth's experience of the mountain. If we list the basic elements in the poem, we obtain at the same time a typology of the fundamental elements in the Sublime.

1. The contrasts between the near and the distant, the earthbound and the striving for the heavens, the limited and the unlimited, chaos and cosmos, darkness and light, distaste and bliss.

2. Meanwhile, these contrasts are not static. The conflict between them generates a rhythmical variation between expansion and contraction, a rising and a sense of being dragged downwards. The overall rhythm is formed as an overriding movement from the constricted to the un-bounded.

3. This ascent is at the same time a transformation in which the normal five senses are replaced by another inner sense opening up an insight into cosmic correspondences, thereby raising the sensory above the concrete and individually limited, to the universal, the divine totality.

The typical and representative content of Wordsworth's *Simplon* poem ought meanwhile not to hide the fact that whereas in the 1790s the young Wordsworth was writing his way into the tradition of the Sublime, he was at the same time adding to it a deeply personal and original interpretation of it, emerging in 1798.

The growth and the structure of this interpretation is the overriding subject of this analysis. But it cannot be derived immediately from *The Simplon*, which comes at the culmination of this vital phase in Wordsworth's development. Through a series of chiefly chronologically ordered considerations of the early work, we shall follow the way in which Wordsworth's understanding of the concept of the Sublime developed and thereby throw some explanatory light on the seemingly traditional sign language of *The Simplon*.

CHAPTER 3

The Inner Light. 1798-1800

> To make the external internal, the internal external,
> to make nature thought, and thought nature –
> this is the mystery of genius in the fine arts.
>
> S.T. Coleridge
> *On Poesy or Art*, 1818

On 25 January 1798, Wordsworth wrote *A Night-Piece*. The poem describes a sublime nature experience, the sight of the unbelievably vast and deep, star-filled heavens. The experience is conveyed in a simple, but characteristic rhythm. The night sky is at first clouded, and the moonlight can only vaguely be discerned. But the clouds gradually disperse, and the lonely wanderer, who has fixed his eyes on the ground and therefore sees nothing, is surprised by sudden bursts of light and looks up. Then he discovers the moon shining brilliant and clear and behind it the star-filled black abyss of the sky, which seems to become ever deeper in its frame of vast cloud formations. At last the vision closes again:

> The sky is overcast
> With a continuous cloud of texture close
> Heavy and wan, all whitened by the Moon,
> Which through that veil is indistinctly seen,
> A dull, contracted circle, yielding light
> So feebly spread that not a shadow falls,
> Chequering the ground – from rock, plant, tree, or tower.
> At length a pleasant instantaneous gleam
> Startles the pensive traveller while he treads
> His lonesome path, with unobserving eye
> Bent earthwards; he looks up – the clouds are split
> Asunder, – and above his head he sees
> The clear Moon, and the glory of the heavens.
> There, in a black-blue vault she sails along,
> Followed by multitudes of stars, that, small
> And sharp, and bright, along the dark abyss
> Drive as she drives: how fast they wheel away,

Yet vanish not! – the wind is in the tree,
But they are silent; – still they roll along
Immeasurably distant; and the vault,
Built round by those white clouds, enormous clouds,
Still deepens its unfathomable depth.
At length the Vision closes; and the mind,
Not undisturbed by the delight it feels,
Which slowly settles into peaceful calm,
Is left to muse upon the solemn scene.
(PW II p.208-209)

The Inner Expansion

The rhythm of these lines is much like labour pains: A rhythm of contraction, expansion, new contraction followed by a new, but now inner, expansion in which a transformation of the consciousness is effected. At first an earthbound, enclosed vision, then an opening to a cosmic perspective and finally a return to the earthbound, but with a contemplative mind that is now filled with peace and delight.[26]

This simple, segmented process is the archetypical pattern for the experience of the Sublime such as we have already seen it in an early, incomplete form – and with a different distribution of the elements – in the alternation between light and dark in the boat poem. *A Night-Piece* is written from a slightly different position, the dark and not the light being the starting point. The lonely – melancholy – wanderer is not, like the young bard, turning away from some threatening darkness, but on the contrary seems tied to it. So the wanderer rather shares the viewpoint with the sober narrator in the boat poem who knows the darkness is there and that it has the last say. But in *A Night-Piece* the darkness is the background to the radical transformation taking place when the universe reveals itself to the wanderer, and he is subsequently raised in his thoughts to a dimension beyond the terrestrial.

In the boat poem the bard manages, despite the darkness, to retain the cosmic experience of the sunset. Now the experience of the cosmic is nature's gift to the wanderer. This important difference in nuance is the first sign of the change in Wordsworth's view of nature which breaks through in earnest in 1798: Nature becomes an actively formative and vital power. As a result of this, the receptive and creative aspects of the imagination are viewed and linked in a completely new way – as will be further demonstrated.

Moreover, darkness and light no longer replace each other in turn, but exist simultaneously as the precondition for each other. The stars and the moonlit clouds serve to emphasise the black abyss of the universe – and vice versa. The difference from the boat poem then lies not in the actual inversion of the relative order of the factors – light and darkness – but in the fact that the dynamic force is external to the person undergoing the experience of nature, and that this nature is constituted by the cosmic dialectic between light and darkness. The experience of the Sublime is correspondingly not a release to the immovable and infinite, but a boundary-crossing experience of the dynamic, simultaneous interaction of the forces.

But this way of experiencing the Sublime contains within it a rhythm that is also dialectic: the constant alternation between the formative effect on and in the receptive *and* creative vision occasioned by impression and meditative recall. In *A Night-Piece* consciousness – fired by the delight awakened by the vision – settles down in meditation on the solemn natural scenery, the experience of the Sublime. It is not as in the boat poem constriction or loss – and the consciousness of death – but the delight at the inner expansion of the vision and mind that forms the starting point for the meditation.

An Ebbing and a Flowing Mind

The key word for this meditative element in the poem is "muse". But the poem does not inform us in more precise terms of what this implies. That is achieved by a number of texts that were written at about the same time as *A Night-Piece*. All revolve around the actual rhythm of contraction and expansion expressed in the adult wanderer's experience of the Sublime, and at the same time this leads Wordsworth back towards fundamental childhood experiences of nature – not necessarily in a narrow biographical sense[27] although a number of central episodes are clearly related to those we shall encounter later in the specifically autobiographical *The Prelude*, 1799.

The main text is the first completed version of *The Pedlar* from February-March 1798, originally intended as part of *The Ruined Cottage*, but now separated off as an independent poem. Here, the writer meets an old man who tells him about his life in the midst of nature as a shepherd boy. The poem opens with a detailed description of how a child's mind is fashioned by intimate association with natural phenomena. The starting point is reminiscent of the situation in *A Night-Piece*: the lonely wanderer and the contrast between cosmic light and darkness:

> He many an evening to his distant home
> In solitude returning saw the hills
> Grow larger in the darkness, all alone
> Beheld the stars come out above his head,
> And travelled through the wood, no comrade near,
> To whom he might confess the things he saw.
> So the foundations of his mind were laid
> In such communion, not from terror free.
> While yet a child, and long before his time
> He had perceived the presence and the power
> Of greatness, and deep feelings had impressed
> Great objects on his mind, with portraiture
> And colour so distinct that on his mind
> They lay like substances, and almost seemed
> To haunt the bodily sense. He had received
> A precious gift, for as he grew in years
> With these impressions would he still compare
> All his ideal stores, his shapes and forms,
> And being still unsatisfied with aught
> Of dimmer character, he thence attained
> An active power to fasten images
> Upon his brain, and on their pictured lines
> Intensely brooded, even till they acquired
> The liveliness of dreams.[28]
> (PW V p.381 ll.71-91)

Wordsworth is not content here merely to note that the foundation of the mind is created in intercourse with a nature that awakens both delight and fear. He tries also to determine how this formative process is effected in a purely factual sense. The sensing of the nearness and power of great nature gives rise to profound feelings which again impress the great natural phenomena on the mind with such force that the images in the mind almost exceed those of the senses. These stored visual impressions are so distinct that he will not be content with anything less in the future.

So he develops the ability actively to retain the images in his mind and meditate on them until they acquire their own autonomous life in the manner of dreams. This aspect is further developed at the end of the first verse of the contemporary fragment *iv* from the *Alfoxden* notebook, written between 20 January and 5 March 1798:

> To gaze
> On that green hill and on those scattered trees
> And feel a pleasant consciousness of life
> In the impression of that loveliness
> Until the sweet sensation called the mind
> Into itself, by image from without
> Unvisited, and all her reflex powers
> Wrapped in a still dream [of] forgetfulness.
> (PW V p.341)

As Wordsworth here describes the way in which the image is formed, there is no question of its being merely the result of impressions received, as Hartley's association psychology would have it, but of the impressions starting a process in the mind which makes it enclose itself in oblivion of itself, beyond the reach of reflection.

With this passage from *The Pedlar* Wordsworth embarks on a determined examination of the imagination and the laws governing it. It is no coincidence that these thoughts emerge in a description of childhood. For it is already obvious now, at least to a reader equipped with the wisdom of hindsight, that it is in the child and the childish mind that the answer to the question of the imagination is to be found. In other words imagination is not a static power, but partakes in the developmental history of each individual. As a consequence of this Wordsworth's interest in childhood takes a completely new turn and assumes greater significance. In *The Pedlar* the first steps were taken towards what was to turn into an autobiographical project covering the whole of his life: *The Prelude*.

The features which Wordsworth isolates in *The Pedlar* are further defined and clarified during 1798 and 1799. As the brief consideration of this text has demonstrated, it is crucial to Wordsworth in this first phase on the one hand to emphasise the fundamental significance of nature impressions and on the other to demonstrate how the ability to fix and form images gradually evolves from the elementary sense impressions. In this way Wordsworth transcends the mechanistic ideas of association psychology. For Wordsworth the image impressed is not merely a mental imprint, for it is infused with a kind of meditative formative power that endows it with its own autonomous mental life. The original sensing survives, then, not merely as an image once and for all received and retained, but as a demanding proto-image filled with feeling and stimulating an active meditative and visionary ability.

This power of metamorphosis which we have encountered as far back as the 1794 passage from *An Evening Walk*, turns out itself to be a stage in a more comprehensive process preparing the boy's mind for a deeper understanding of the essence of nature and his relationship with it:

> But he had felt the power
> Of nature, and already was prepared
> By his intense conceptions to receive
> Deeply the lesson of love, which he
> Whom Nature, by whatever means, has taught
> To feel intensely, cannot but receive.
> (PW V pp.382 ll.112-117)

Fundamentally, the power of nature is love, i.e. an infinite and all-encompassing relationship, not in a static but in a dynamic sense: a dialectic between independent parties such as love by definition unfolds. Yet another fragment from the *Alfoxden* notebook treats this sublime dialectic:

> Of unknown modes of being which on earth,
> Or in the heavens, or in the heavens and earth
> Exist by mighty combinations, bound
> Together by a link, and with a soul
> Which makes all one.
> (PW V p.340-341)

To experience this living relationship is for the nine-year-old boy in *The Pedlar* to experience God as the power residing in all things. This happens when, from a vantage point between heaven and earth, the boy sees the world revealed before his eyes bathed in the cosmic light of the sun.

> Oh! then what soul was his when on the tops
> Of the high mountains he beheld the sun
> Rise up and bathe the world in light. He looked,
> The ocean and the earth beneath him lay
> In gladness and deep joy. The clouds were touched
> And in their silent faces did he read
> Unutterable love.
> (PW V p.382 ll.122-128)

Here, in this primal scene, the experience of the sun in the old boat poem is retained but with a significant difference. Now it is the rising sun that disperses the darkness and lights the universe and the sensing boy. The core of this sublime experience is meditative in kind just as in the previous poem, but Wordsworth makes it clear that at the same time a transformation is taking place in the receptive mind.

> Sound needed none
> Nor any voice of joy: his spirit drank
> The spectacle. Sensation, soul and form
> All melted into him. They swallowed up
> His animal being;[29]
> (PW V p.382 ll.128-132)

As almost always with Wordsworth, the transition takes place in a state marked by loneliness and quiet, originating in the boy's own active spirit drinking in the vision – a metaphor which plays a central part in *The Prelude*, 1799. In this process the boy becomes the object of a force that implants in him the experience as well as the spirit and form of which the experience is the vehicle. And this incorporation leads to a suspension of what at first was the boy's spontaneous, instinctively acting self. Its place is taken by the formative forces that are present in the vision.

The transformation is determined by the fusing of the mind with the incursive cosmic force – the sunlight. This spiritualisation or enlightenment of the self is not the contribution of individual thought and reflection, but of the incorporation of the cosmic conditions into feeling thereby lending form to the emotions. The expansive power intervenes in the mind of the poet and releases it, making it commensurate with great all-pervasive nature. The poem then continues with these words:

                    in them did he live
            And by them did he live. They were his life.
            In such access of mind, in such high hour
            Of visitation from the living God,
            He did not feel the God; he felt his works;
            Thought was not. In enjoyment it expired.
            (PW V p.382 ll.132-137)

Sublime joy presupposes the suspension of thought. In his emotional
willingness to receive the god in his creation, the experiencing boy's very
being becomes sublime and comprehensive. The divine power acting from
outside finds its complement in the boy's spontaneous self-realisation:

            What wonder if his being thus became
            Sublime and comprehensive.
            (PW V p.383 ll.156-157)

The sense of the Sublime, which here reveals itself as comprising the
highest human values, is then an effect of the Sublime itself as an objective cosmic force – the soul which makes everything one in the *Alfoxden*
fragment quoted above; or as is said at the end of the *Alfoxden* fragment
ii: "In all forms of things/ There is a mind". This is the consciousness to
which the self opens itself and by which it is formed in its meditative
absorption in great nature.

In the early months of 1798 Wordsworth was engrossed in this meditative
form of experience and its unexploited possibilities. This is confirmed by
a number of fragments from the *Alfoxden* notebook, especially numbers
i and *iv*. The first describes how cosmic light – as in *A Night-Piece* – that
of the moon, penetrates via the sight into the soul and the heart in the
sensing subject:

                there would he stand
            In the still covert of some (?lonesome) rock,
            Or gaze upon the moon until its light
            Fell like a strain of music on his soul[30]
            and seem'd to sink into his very heart.
            (PW V p.340)

It is the same intense, meditative gaze that is the starting point of fragment *iv*, which was discussed above. If we read the next verse along with it, it becomes clear that the meditative process forms part of a greater rhythm, an alternation between on the one hand a consciousness of self and the surrounding world and on the other the mind's self-forgetting embrace of the impression.

>   To gaze
> On that green hill and on those scattered trees
> And feel a pleasant consciousness of life
> In the impression of that loveliness
> Until the sweet sensation called the mind
> Into itself, by image from without
> Unvisited, and all her reflex powers
> Wrapped in a still dream (of) forgetfulness.
>
> I lived without the knowledge that I lived
> Then by those beauteous forms brought back again
> To lose myself again as if my life
> Did ebb and flow with a strange mystery.
> (PW V p.341)

Wordsworth here focuses sharply on the transitional state which is the pivotal point of the meditative, sublime experience of nature. So the poet vacillates between a state in which the subject and object are distinct from each other – and the world like the poet himself is the object of the poet's reflection – and then a fundamentally different state of pure, unreflective being from which he is then awakened only to sink back into it again. But this vacillation is not a result of the poet's will, it is produced by a cosmic rhythm to which he is subjected and which Wordsworth also calls love. What in the 1789 boat poem was an indissoluble succession of unity and separation, is here part of an unceasing dialectic which neutralises the loss, though at the same time it also implies that the unity or fusion is not definitive, but is placed both in the past and the future. The Sublime is thus tied to the actual process, the dialectic – not to a perpetual state.

In contrast to the nature experiences in *The Pedlar*, the experience of nature here cannot be classified as sublime on the basis of the conventional aesthetical criteria of the time, as it does not derive from the experience of grandiose scenery, but rather of beautiful, picturesque scenery – the green hill and the scattered trees. Nevertheless, it shows the same fundamental characteristics as the sublime experience: the unreflective, meditative experience of the fusion with the mystic power expressed in the dialectic between contraction and expansion.

Wordsworth's own interpretation of the experience as sublime and not picturesque, is due to the fact that for him nature – understood as the cosmic power or consciousness existing in all things – reveals its greatness irrespective of its outward appearance, for the very reason that greatness depends on nature as an active force, not on isolated and limited phenomena. This is why the mind, once formed by great nature, can experience the Sublime even in its unspectacular, everyday guise as in the present case where the cosmic power expresses itself in the life of the self as a rhythmical ebb and flow. In this perspective there is at least one important but apparently under-emphasised premise for Wordsworth's declared programme in *Lyrical Ballads*, most clearly put in the preface to the second edition, 1800: to make the simple life into the subject of poetry. This is expressed in the following passage:

> The principal object, then, proposed in these Poems was to choose incidents and situations from common life, and to relate or describe them, throughout, as far as was possible in a selection of language really used by men, and at the same time, to throw over them a certain colouring of imagination, whereby ordinary things should be presented to the mind in an unusual aspect.
> (PW II p.386)

This social sphere appears to represent a source of elementary human nature and its elevated potential in the same way as childhood:

> Humble and rustic life was generally chosen, because, in that condition, the essential passions of the heart find a better soil in which they can attain their maturity (...) because (...) our elementary feelings coexist in a state of greater simplicity (...) and, lastly, because in that condition the passions of men are incorporated with the beautiful and permanent forms of Nature.
> (PW II pp.386-387)

So in its basic intention *Lyrical Ballads* is part and parcel of Wordsworth's general search for the Sublime in nature untouched by man. Thus – for instance – the cosmic orderliness expressed in man's elementary being is described in almost the same words in fragment *iv* and *The Pedlar*. The difference is that whereas in the fragment the poet senses the mystical power in his own life, the boy in *The Pedlar* observes it as a power which in general controls the life of nature:

> He traced an ebbing and a flowing mind,
> Expression ever varying.
> (PW V p.382 ll.107-108)

What the boy observes outside himself is the same divine consciousness as that which expresses itself in the individual, receptive mind. In other *Alfoxden* fragments there is also, as we have seen, a question of the consciouness or soul that is present in all things. Fragment *ii*: "In all forms of things/There is a mind" and fragment *iii*: "a soul/Which makes all one". (PW V pp.340-341)

Introspection is Retrospection

From this examination of the child's sublime experience of unity let us return to our starting point, the idea of "musing" as it appears in the final line of *A Night-Piece*: "to muse upon that solemn scene". For it is not sufficient merely to characterise this activity as meditative.

As we have already seen "musing" implies reflection and thus has a reflective character in contrast to the child's/boy's spontaneous meditative evolution in the prevoiusly treated texts. *A Night-Piece* is indeed about an adult form of consciousness. Nevertheless, there is no question of reflection here in the sense of the workings of a purely analytic, detached intellect. The difference between the consciousness of the child and that of the adult could be described by distinguishing between primary spontaneous, and secondary willed meditation which then again can be contrasted with meditation as an analytical and reflective effort.

The portrayal of the child in *The Pedlar* shows that meditation develops according to a logic built into the original experience of nature. It is not the boy who decides, but "these impressions" which compel him to develop an active ability to retain impressions and nurse them until they acquire their own life in his mind.

This involuntary behaviour is something the adult can take over as a paradigm which can also work on the premises of reflection. The paradigmatic element in the child's behaviour, then, depends on the child's spontaneous, retrospective way of experiencing – the boy nursing his impressions – being an elementary form of conscious adult retrospection. The adult's meditative engagement in nature and experience of the unity of all things is in that way a repetition – conscious or not – of the child's original experience and way of experiencing. As will be seen, Wordsworth expands this idea not least in *The Prelude*, 1799, but also in later poems such as *My heart leaps up* and *To the Cuckoo*, both from 1802.

The so-called *Christabel* manuscript contains several fragments from 1798, including one numbered *vi*, in which Wordsworth explicitly describes the adult's meditative experience as an interplay between introspection and retrospection. The trance-like openness to nature impressions leads to the mind's becoming absorbed in itself and consequently to possible self-understanding.

> In many a walk
> At evening or by moonlight, or reclined
> At midday upon beds of forest moss,
> Have we to nature and her impulses
> Of our whole being made free gift, and when
> Our trance had left us, oft have we, by aid
> Of the impressions which it left behind,
> Looked inward on ourselves, and learned perhaps,
> Something of what we are.
> (PW V pp.343-344 ll.8-16)

As has already been argued, this introspection is at the same time a retrospection in which the original impressions of delight are recalled to renewed life.

> Nor in those hours
> Did we destroy [   ]
> The original impression of delight,
> But by such retrospect it was recalled
> To yet a second and a second life,
> While in excitation of the mind
> A vivid pulse of sentiment and thought
> Beat palpably within us, and all shades
> Of consciousness were ours.
> (PW V p.344 ll.16-24)

In this process the pattern founded upon the child's reworking of nature impressions is repeated. Thus it is specially in retrospection, recalling the initial impression that consciousness grows and is changed. What survives and is recalled in retrospection, however, is not the original impression of delight as a "picture" fixed once and for all, neither in the child nor in the adult. From *The Pedlar* and the *Alfoxden* fragments on, the impressions received have been conceived as an added potential for change. This potential is brought to fruition when, as here, the mind is inspired on recalling the experience, and the consciousness expands in the pulsation shared by thought and feeling. In the sublime experience the mature mind is put into the same emotional and visionary state as was that of the child.

The crucial factor in this expansion of the consciousness ("all shades of consciousness") is, however, that even in the case of the adult is it not the self but imprinted nature that is the active, formative force. So in keeping with the texts just examined, the pulse beating in the "excitation" of the mind cannot be seen as that of the person remembering either, but as yet another manifestation of what Wordsworth calls the cosmic variation between ebb and flow. In this elementary accord between consciousness and nature the child's way of experiencing becomes manifest as the very foundation for that of the adult.

The Mind of Man
"To muse", then, can be defined as the expansion of the grown poet's imagination formed on the basis of the child's spontaneous experience of grand, sublime nature. The word "formed" implies two separate states. Firstly – as we have seen it in the texts from the early months of 1798 – the imagination is formed by early nature impressions and their repercussions on the child's mind; secondly, via introspection and retrospection, the adult poet can awaken this latent impressed form and let it act formatively and creatively.

The way to the Sublime may well start in the earliest experiences of wonderful and dangerous nature – but it continues in the inner regions of the mind thus formed. Only in the visionary and creative act are the potential insights released which are built into the child's original sublime experience of nature.

As early as in *The Pedlar* Wordsworth attempts from this point of view to draw consequences of principle. This is done in a lengthy reflective passage added to the first version of the poem and spoken by the old man. It starts with the thought that nature is not only what is physically present, but also a metaphor, perhaps, for the highest things:

> Or was it ever meant
> That this majestic imagery, the clouds
> The ocean and the firmament of heaven
> Should lie a barren picture on the mind?
> (PW V p.402 ll.68-71)

More clearly than anywhere else in the early 1798 texts it can be seen here that the immediate visual impression of nature encompasses another image presupposing the ability to have visions of an entirely different kind. Wordsworth calls it "That other eye" in the 1794 fragment and describes it as creative in fragment *iv* of the *Christabel* manuscript, 1798. Later, in the B manuscript of *The Ruined Cottage* from 1800, he talks of the "eye within" (PW V p.400 1. passage) and in *I Wandered Lonely*, 1804, of "the inward eye" (PW II p.217 1.21)). It is this awakening of spiritual sight by the physical experience that Wordsworth sketches in the introductory portrait of the meditating boy in *The Pedlar*.

In an addendum to the B manuscript of *The Ruined Cottage*, Wordsworth goes further and bases an entire pattern for awakening on man's possibility of rising above the customary blindness to existing nature and awakening to the comprehensive unity of which both the phenomenon of nature and man are part:

> Let us rise
> From this oblivious sleep, these fretful dreams
> Of feverish nothingness. Thus disciplined
> All things shall live in us and we shall live
> In all things that surround us.
> (PW V p.402 ll.76-80)

Form and feeling, senses and "intellect", phenomenon and consciousness are woven together into an indissoluble dialectic:

For thus the senses and the intellect
Shall each to each supply a mutual aid,
Invigorate and sharpen and refine
Each other with a power that knows no bound,
And forms and feelings acting thus, and thus
Reacting, they shall each acquire
A living spirit and a character
Till then unfelt, and each be multiplied
With a variety that knows no end.
(PW V p.402 ll.83-91)

The object of this process is to open both the senses and the consciousness to an ever more comprehensive insight into man's inner nature. For this is where the key to an understanding of external nature is hidden.

What'er we see
What'er we feel, by agency direct
Or indirect, shall tend to feed and nurse
Our faculties, and raise to loftier heights
Our intellectual soul.
(PW V p.403 ll.95-99)

The senses must be fed and the intellect uplifted in one sweep. However, there is no question simply of a metaphorical transfer to man of the qualities of sublime, cosmic nature. A remarkable feature in Wordsworth's writing during these years is that his concern with human consciousness is not a self-centred, solipsistic one. The world, nature, is not a projection of the individual consciousness, but is its inescapable foundation. Man's inner eye is the sense or the understanding fashioned by cosmic nature. This has consequences for the view of human consciousness and its sublime dimension. If man can experience the Sublime, it is – as Wordsworth presupposes in *The Pedlar* – because the Sublime already exists in man as a potential, a latent dynamic ingredient in his consciousness, founded upon the impression of grand nature.

So from this coincidence springs a fundamental dialectic between the individual consciousness and the physical world: The external and the internal are both valid forms of expression for the same nature, i.e. all-embracing consciousness. As Wordsworth formulates it in fragments *ii* and *iii* from the *Alfoxden* notebook: "In all forms of life/There is a mind".

Everything in existence is "bound/Together with a link, and with a soul/ Which makes all one". (PW V pp.340-341) This fundamental identity is the explanation of how the perceived image contains a deeper truth than can immediately be grasped by the senses, but which feeling – and consequently the meditative re-call – can capture. The adult meditative, visionary practice thus derives strength from the emotions to dissolve the boundary between the outer and inner and between the individual consciousness and the cosmic consciousness ("mind").

This dissolution of boundaries is the very essence of the sublime experience. We have met it right back in the additions to *An Evening Walk*, where all boundaries are blurred; now Wordsworth presents the meditative dissolution of boundaries not merely as a suspension, but as a metamorphosis implying the melting of the boundary between inner and outer, as here in fragment *iii* from the *Christabel* manuscript:

> Oh 'tis a joy divine on summer days
> When not a breeze is stirring, not a cloud,
> To sit within some solitary wood,
> Far in some lonely wood, and hear no sound
> Which the heart does not make, or else so fit(s)
> To its own temper that in external things
> No longer seem internal difference
> All melts away, and things that are without
> Live in our minds as in their native home.[31]
> (PW V p.343)

In line with the previously quoted passage from *The Pedlar* ("All melted into him" (PW V p.382 l.131)), the key word to this crossing of boundaries, "melt", means the dissolution of the normal boundaries between outer and inner, making the mind an abode for the phenomena of the external world. Only here do they find their real, original meaning, understood in the sense that the external phenomenon is united with the original impressed form.

In contrast to the old boat poem of 1787, Wordsworth in the first months of 1798 seems to imagine that the fall accompanying the growth of man's ability to reflect can be warded off by that ability being referred back to the universal nature from which it has emerged. The idea is that the lost relationship has not been lost in a profound sense. It is still present in elementary reality but either hidden or disavowed because man is the prisoner of his senses (as the young person often is) or of his intellectual vanity (as is the adult).

This vanity of the intellect is something which Wordsworth firmly confronts in the dialogue poem *Expostulation and Reply* (written May 1798) and the related monologic programme poem *The Tables Turned* (written 1798), published one after the other in *Lyrical Ballads*, 1798. In the first of the two the character called Matthew taunts his counterpart William for his dreamy, vegetative attitude to the world, but receives the reply from William that nature contains forces that impress themselves uninvited on the receptive mind:

> I deem that there are Powers
> Which of themselves our minds impress;
> That we can feed this mind of ours
> In a wise passiveness.
> (PW IV p.56 ll.21-24)

Wordsworth opposes this attitude in the following poem with the negative view, the self-sufficient and self-aware ability to reflect:

> Our meddling intellect
> Mis-shapes the beauteous forms of things:
> We murder to dissect.
> (PW IV p.57 ll.26-28)

There is Creation in the Eye

The problem of reconciling consciousness and nature, however, was not to be solved that easily. The *Lines written a few miles above Tintern Abbey*, dated 13 July 1798, are crucial evidence of this. In both theme and composition the poem makes explicit the unexpressed duality characteristic of all the texts from the beginning of 1798. They are retrospective descriptions of an experience of unity. So as he writes, or tells, about it, the poet finds himself in a reflective position beyond the fusion of the two.

This very aspect appears in the composition of the poem. The narrator alternates between depicting the landscape now and as it used to be, while at the same time introducing himself as experiencing in both the present and the past. The past is both the concrete landscape which the narrator experienced then and is now seeing again, and also the self that experienced it. The distinction between them is made necessary by the renewed meeting revealing that an important change has taken place. For while the landscape is unchanged, the narrator discovers that *he* is not the same as he was then. The joyous reunion with the unchanged landscape is at the same time a melancholy realisation of a completed inner transformation which can be interpreted both as the loss of immediacy and as intellectual growth.

What at first looks like a nostalgic return is therefore really the narrator's reflection on his special relationship with the landscape. The loss turns out to be an unavoidable prerequisite for the process the poet has undergone since leaving the landscape. This ambiguity is reflected in the poem's alternation between a past that is recalled and a present that is experienced.

The poem starts in the present. From that position it is possible to discern two levels of past experience. The first takes us back to the time following the original experience and describes how the "forms of beauty" in the landscape have lived on in the spectator's consciousness, where they have brought "sensations sweet" in their wake, sensations which soothe or are transformed into kindly and gentle actions. But most important of all is the fact that the embedded forms of beauty and feelings have given birth to another, more sublime, blissful mental state in the spectator which ultimately results in his becoming purified soul. With greater artistic precision than in the preceding descriptions of the introspective, meditative experience, Wordsworth here reveals how another faculty of vision grows in the individual, while the material eye at the same time is calmed down and the inner life of the phenomena are contemplated:

> the affections gently lead us on,
> Until, the breath of this corporeal frame,
> And even the motion of our human blood
> Almost suspended, we are laid asleep
> In body, and become a living soul;
> While with an eye made quiet by the power
> Of harmony, and the deep power of joy,
> We see into the life of things.
> (PW II p.260 ll.42-49)

At this juncture, where in its confrontation with the actual landscape the self has contemplated its own transformation, the other level of the past emerges. It takes us a step further back to the actual experience of the landscape that left "the picture of the mind", that is to say back to the person he was at the time when it was impressed in him, but which he no longer is. However he is not capable of describing his past self because he was exclusively defined by his spontaneous, unreflected, sensuous existence in nature. His past identity not being divorced from nature he was therefore not yet a self.

>   – – – I cannot paint
> What then I was. The sounding cataract
> Haunted me like a passion, the tall rock,
> The mountain, and the deep and gloomy wood,
> Their colours and their forms, were then to me
> An appetite; a feeling and a love,
> That had no need of a remoter charm,
> By thought supplied, nor any interest
> Unborrowed from the eye.[32]
> (PW II p.261 ll.75-83)

This description of the poet five years previously[33] reveals that what the writer presently deems sublime was originally the result of unreflecting, immediate sensing, an elementary appetite for nature.

Nature's having sublime characteristics does not, then – in keeping with the texts from the beginning of 1798 – derive from the elements in nature simply acting as symbols of the boy's mind, but from nature's actually being sublime, impressing itself on his mind. As we already know from the earlier texts, the adult's experience of the Sublime is made possible through these impressions – the fashioning of the mind that takes place in the child's early, unreflecting experience of grand physical nature. The sublime mind is thus the product of this sublime nature, and every subsequent – i.e. adult or reflective – experience of the Sublime is for the same reason both a confirmation and a reexperience.

In *Lines written a few miles above Tintern Abbey*, Wordsworth is, however, not content to incorporate his thoughts so far on the Sublime. He goes further. For the initial forming of the mind is viewed in a different perspective than in the texts from 1798 read so far. As already stated, the poem is about a loss. This means that two essentially different experiences of unity appear in it: the original, unreflecting experience which the narrator is remembering, and then the indirect, presupposing the consciousness of what was once unconscious and is now transformed into the words of the poem. The loss is therefore not simply a loss, an unproductive deficiency; it is also the necessary precondition for the emergence of other abilities and insights than those of the child.

> other gifts
> Have followed for such loss, I would believe,
> Abundant recompence. For I have learned
> To look on nature, not as in the hour
> Of thoughtless youth; (...)
> (...)
> And I have felt
> A presence that disturbs me with the joy
> Of elevated thoughts; a sense sublime
> Of something far more deeply interfused,
> Whose dwelling is the light of setting suns,
> And the round ocean, and the living air,
> And the blue sky, and in the mind of man,
> A motion and a spirit that impels
> All thinking things, all objects of all thought,
> And rolls through all things.
> (PW II p.261 ll.86-90 and 93-102)

The loss of the self-forgetful, physical experience of unity is counterbalanced by qualities of consciousness providing a cosmic insight into the nature that simply presented itself immediately to the senses of the child or the youth. Consequently the youth's original experience of the Sublime is repeated for the adult on a fundamentally different level at which the individual has divorced himself in feeling and thought from the grand phenomena and begins to sense that they are manifestations of a power and an intellect that infuses and combines everything in nature and the human mind.

Instead of the original unreflecting unity with nature appears an insight into the powers connecting the person experiencing and the experience itself. This process of making conscious does not, however, lead to alienation; on the contrary it represents the reason for the poet's having retained his original love of nature. It is still a totality, it is still the foundation for his existence. Being inseperable from the dynamics of change set by nature, sublimity does not disappear simply because the individual has changed:

> Therefore am I still
> A lover of the meadows and the woods,
> And mountains; and of all that we behold
> From this green earth; of all the mighty world
> Of eye and ear, – both what they half create,
> And what perceive; well pleased to recognize
> In nature and the language of the sense
> The anchor of my purest thoughts, the nurse,
> The guide, the guardian of my heart, and soul
> Of all my moral being.[34]
> (PW II p.262 ll. 102-111)

To this point of view nature, i.e. elementary nature, is the firm ground beneath the poet's thoughts, feelings and entire moral being. Not as the result of passive, mechanical mirroring, but of a dialectic between external influences on the senses and the internal ordering of those impressions. This dialectic Wordsworth suggests as far back as in the dual significance of "touches soft" in the 1794 fragment's description of the reflective surface of the lake, and in the description in *The Ruined Cottage* of how the sense impressions form the way in which the person sensing actually senses. The senses are at one and the same time both receptive, organs for recording, and formative because they have themselves been formed. Their role as formative agents is emphasised in fragment *vi* from the *Christabel* notebook:

> There is creation in the eye,
> Nor less in all the other senses; powers
> They are that colour, model, and combine
> The things perceived with such an absolute
> Essential energy that we may say
> That those most godlike faculties of ours
> At one and the same moment are the mind
> And the mind's minister.
> (PW V p.343)

But this does not imply that the senses are arbitrarily – subjectively – creative. The fundamental realisation in *Tintern Abbey* is that what is sensed, that with which it is sensed and the person sensing are not mutually distinct entities, but manifestations of one and the same cosmic nature – "A motion and a spirit that impels/All thinking things, all objects of all thought,/And rolls through all things". What the spiritual eye creates as it senses is not another nature than that which is. For what it creates, it creates exactly because it was created by this all-pervading cosmic spirit. In this respect creative sensing corresponds to the "thought-less" understanding which is that of the child.

The Time of Unrememberable Being

So *Lines written a few miles above Tintern Abbey* is a grandiose attempt at bringing together and expanding the reflections on the relationship between nature and consciousness in the preceding poems. But as he focuses on the retrospective via the meditative experience, Wordsworth inevitably sharpens his own awareness not only of what links or unites, but also what divides the child's and the adult's experience of the oneness of nature. It is this latter element – the difference between the person writing and the person being written about – that Wordsworth pursues further in the second half of 1798. And he does so with a growing awareness that the picture of the boy's world in *The Pedlar* is part of a far more extensive poetical project than the poem from which it originated.

There are signs of this process in the series of fragments written during October and November 1798. They are found in the so-called *JJ* manuscript and together form the essence of what in edited and expanded form constitutes the first part of *The Prelude* of 1799. The two-part poem was mainly written between October 1798 and January 1799 and again between October and December 1799, when the copy of the whole work was completed.

To avoid unnecessary repetition in my discussion of the first part, I have chosen to limit myself to the final text of 1799. In the case of important divergences in content, the earlier fragments will be included in the discussion.

As in *The Pedlar* and *Tintern Abbey*, Wordsworth's path to a deeper understanding of the relationship between consciousness and nature goes via memory and imagination. But he chooses to look much further back in his own past and to begin on the level where the child has still not acquired a language. The narrator who is telling of himself as a child is, like the first-person writer in *Tintern Abbey*, aware of his position as an adult and the gulf thus separating him from what he once was. But at the same time it is his ambition to discover the link that in fact exists between the child and the adult – not despite, but because of, the difference and the separation.

The Prelude, 1799, contains what broadly speaking can be called two "genres". They can be identified as two different narrators or narrative positions as far back as in the boat poem of 1787. One is the intense portrayal of tangible episodes with emphasis put on the experience of the senses and the emotions (in the boat poem: the experience of the water, first lit by the sun and then black). The other is the generalised consideration of the circumstances applying (in the boat poem: the writer's reflections on the young bard's insistence on remembering the bright colours).

These two attitudes are constitutive of *The Prelude*, 1799. Partly as a visionary recall of the child's experiences, world and consciousness, and partly as a reflection on the actual imagination and its connection with both what is imagined and the person imagining. The two positions seem to correspond to a dynamic poetical strategy in which the meditative, visionary remembrance of the original experience opens up for reflection, which then for its part can make way for new, related visions. The composition of the first part is evidence of this. Certainly the autobiographical central figure in the poem gradually becomes older but this biological and psychological chronology is not the main principle of coherence. It rather stems from the fact that Wordsworth just like the adult narrator himself becomes more and more enlightened as the glimpses of memory accumulate and he is able to reflect on them. In this sense the poem seems in all important respects to mirror the stages in his own developmental process and the poet's evolving insight into the relationship between nature and consciousness.[35] •

The Prelude, 1799, begins in the same way as *Tintern Abbey* with the speaker being confronted with a landscape or an element in such a

61

landscape – in this case the River Derwent – and moving back in memory to the child's very earliest relationship to this landscape. The waters of the river flowing through it all are in *The Prelude*, 1799, a manifestation of the cosmic as an all-embracing, formative power – in Wordsworth's own words from *Tintern Abbey:* "A motion and a spirit that (...) rolls through all things". In writing "manifestation" rather than image or symbol, I want to emphasise Wordsworth's insistence on the cosmic as a concrete natural phenomenon.[36] The river, which for the adult writer is a physical reality, was also a reality for the child. But the cosmic reveals itself in different ways depending on who senses it. In the world of a tiny child – as Wordsworth well knows – it is not vision but hearing that is the primary sense: the murmuring of the river is interwoven with the nurse's singing and the child's dreams in a state in which there is no distinction between the self and the surrounding world:

> the fairest of all rivers, loved
> To blend his murmurs with my nurse's song,
> (...)
> And from his fords and shallows, sent a voice
> That flowed along my dreams?
> (N p.1 ll.2-3 and 5-6)

In four lines included in the 1798 fragment but omitted from *The Prelude*, 1799, Wordsworth emphasises that this turning back to his very earliest life does not lead to a nostalgic embellishment, although the period in question is the child's unreflecting, wordless communion with nature:

> – and now I speak of things
> That have been, and that are, no gentle dreams
> Complacent fashioned fondly to adorn
> The time of unrememberable being.
> (N p.487 ll.16-19)

The grown poet's ambition on the other hand is to give expression to this very early, unrememberable time when the boy and the phenomena of nature cannot be separated: the water both flows through his inner being and embraces his body. The introductory passage of *The Prelude*, 1799, culminates in the four-year-old boy, who is quite literally bathing in cosmos – the water, the sun and the great expanses of the earth – being confirmed from above in his link with nature in what seems to be the heavenly baptism of the naked creature of nature by nature itself: "A naked savage in the thunder-shower". (N p.1, l.26)

The initiation turns out to be a new stage in the development of the child's relationship with nature, inevitably leading to the disintegration of the total unity with nature experienced in early childhood. This happens in a series of episodes in which the boy sets out into nature, discovering and interfering, hunting woodcock and stealing from traps only to be pursued by the footsteps of invisible beings who rule out there. The close relationship with nature now appears to the reader in the form of a clear dialectic. At the same time as the young conqueror and explorer penetrates still further into a nature that is grand but not entirely safe, these beings manifest themselves as spirits or quiet powers that secretly lead him but occasionally also reveal themselves. As the narrator puts it at a philosophical distance:

> I believe
> That there are spirits which, when they would form
> A favoured being, from his very dawn
> Of infancy do open out the clouds
> As at the touch of lightening, seeking him
> With gentle visitation – quiet powers,
> (...)
> With me, though rarely, in my boyish days
> They communed.
> (N p.3 ll.69-77)

Unheeded by the boy himself, these elementary forces reveal themselves in his very earliest life through the waters of the river and then in the rain of the thunderstorm – the waters of birth and baptism respectively – which then with a characteristic Wordsworthian double meaning become "the river of my mind", the remembered river and the mind's river in one, corresponding – as we have already seen – to the cosmic being discovered as an "impressed" reality or form within the conscious mind of the grown man.

When the boy becomes conscious of nature as a world distinct from his own body and will, it first reveals itself as enigmatic forces controlling his life. On the one hand he experiences that nature is not limited to its immediate physical manifestations and he develops into an unconscious and primitive metaphysician – nature appears to the consciousness as something more than just a completely physical presence. There is something "in", "behind" or "above" it. On the other hand his consciousness is not yet of a reflective kind, but is still based on spontaneous impressions of the basic elements in physical nature: mountains, wind and sky.

This is confirmed by one of the boy's earliest lone expeditions into the inaccessible and grand mountain landscape: "In the high places, on the lonesome peaks,/Among the mountains and the winds". (N p.2 ll.54-55) The passage portrays the elementary, cosmic countryside – and thus the Sublime. But in so doing it also reveals how this nature impresses its mighty, grandiose forms on the boy who has clambered up to reach the raven's nest and is now hanging up above it in imminent danger of falling into the depths.

The boy is no longer purely and simply a naked savage, at one with the rain. As in the case of the hunter, nature is not something with which he is inextricably woven together, plain and simple. The first separation has taken place, consequently nature is now also an adversary that has to be conquered. But although the boy's dealings with this adversary are governed by his immediate need for competition, excitement and new discoveries, his behaviour is unconsciously directed towards a higher goal. For the forces that have surfaced in him must not be confused with their immediate expression:

> Though mean
> And though inglorious were my views, the end
> Was not ignoble. Oh, when I have hung
> Above the raven's nest, by knots of grass
> Or half-inch fissures in the slipp'ry rock
> But ill sustained, and almost, as it seemed,
> Suspended by the blast which blew amain,
> Shouldering the naked crag, oh, at that time,
> While on the perilous ridge I hung alone,
> With what strange utterance did the loud dry wind
> Blow through my ears; the sky seemed not a sky
> Of earth, and with what motion moved the clouds!
> (N p.2-3 ll.55-66)

By conquering fear and the physical obstacles the boy raises himself above earthly nature. As he overcomes the elementary constraining forces, he becomes one with the sky and the drifting clouds in a blissful and supreme sense of hovering. The separation between him and the natural elements is resolved into a superior union. Without the boy himself being aware of it, this experience takes place in the form of a crossing of boundaries, a form obeying the very same pattern as the total identification with nature in his early childhood.

Seen through the eyes of the adult narrator, the boy's joyful sense of hovering does not merely point backwards towards the child's very first experience of unity, but also forward towards the adult's own experiences of the Sublime, which in this way appear as a temporary final stage in a long process of articulation and transformation, involving the constant interchange between nature and consciousness. What is repeated and at the same time appears in a new form to the boy at the raven's nest is not a concrete experience, but a fundamental pattern of experience, a form of consciousness that disposes him and later the adult to intellectual and moral greatness. The recurrent elements in this form of consciousness are arranged in a quite specific, rhythmical order: first the individual's involuntary attraction towards what transcends the normal boundaries, then the search for that which has never before been experienced and finally the joy resulting from having conquered new ground for a self who now looks on the world through changed eyes.

In the actual experience this joy is linked to the fact that the boy has revealed himself to be physically and psychologically stronger than gravity and his own fear. The outer achievement gives birth to or turns into an inner ascent or expansion. Precisely this movement from external sensuousness to internal intellectuality is the essence in the sublime experience as known also to Wordsworth's contemporaries.

The Beatings of the Heart

The fascinating aspect of Wordsworth's presentation of the Sublime here is however, not this external structural agreement as such, but the divergencies from the conventional conception of the Sublime contained in the poems from 1798-1799. On the one hand Wordsworth portrays the Sublime as a form of consciousness with its own genesis in the human psyche, and on the other he links this to the development of the individual in his life together with and in nature. The adult experience of the Sublime, the inner expansion is – from the point of view of the remembering poet – formed on the basis of the child's very earliest experience of being inextricably bound up with nature. In the child's elementary experience of its ties with nature – in the time of unrememberable being – we are thus presented with the Sublime in the forms existing before consciousness and language – and accordingly with the fundamental pattern which *The Prelude,* 1799, both explores and is based on.

However, as we have encountered them for instance in the boy robbing the nest, these early sublime experiences are not limited to the experience of unity. The child's euphoric re-experiencing of the unity presupposes his incipient separation from the original closeness to nature. And in this separation a hitherto unknown sense of alienation and exposure invades the boy's relationship with nature.[37] One evening the gentle, hidden powers suddenly reveal another sinister aspect when the boy sets out alone in a boat on the moonlit waters. Here he experiences his own emotions by reversing the order of things: The cliffs ahead of him come threateningly towards him, and finally he has to flee from them – in much the same way as after the theft from the trap, but with profounder consequences corresponding to his having become older. What from the boy's point of view appears as an expulsion from a hitherto kindly, familiar nature is to an adult mind the boy's own – unconscious – doing. His penetration of nature separates him from his immediate, vegetative life close to it, and it becomes alien.[38]

> There was a darkness – call it solitude,
> Or blank desertion – no familiar shapes
> Of hourly objects, images of trees,
> Of sea or sky, no colours of green fields,
> But huge and mighty forms that do not live
> Like living men moved slowly through my mind
> By day, and were the trouble of my dreams.
> (N p.4 ll.123-129)

So day and night he is plagued by ideas that do not as hitherto correspond to outer, temporal, recognisable objects, but rather seem to have their roots in a darkness, a loneliness and a sense of desertion.

The Sublime here lies in the indefinable, the dimly perceived, the threateningly alien, not as fullness and fulfilment. Seen in the overall context of *The Prelude*, this emptiness is not definitive, but a necessary pole in the dialectic which the sublime pattern of experiences works on in the child. Its evolution is based on this pattern of contradictions, fear and delight. Thus the alienation and the darkness are dialectically linked to the experience of fullness and light – exactly as in the case of the lonely adult wanderer in *A Night-Piece*.

The experience of alienation is the launch into the unknown and the inscrutable, which must of necessity precede the sublime delight in the unity of all things and the conquest of new territories in the consciousness. But alienation also inevitably follows upon the experience of unity, thereby forcing a new attempt to cross boundaries. This rhythmical regularity in the dialectic between fear and delight, contraction and expansion, which *A Night-Piece* expresses poetically, receives its first overall formulation in *The Prelude* in a passage that adopts and weaves together the preceding descriptions of how the child's feelings are woven together with elevated, imperishable phenomena:[39]

> Ah, not in vain ye beings of the hills,
> And ye that walk the woods and open heaths
> By moon or star-light, thus, from my first dawn
> Of childhood, did ye love to intertwine
> The passions that build up our human soul
> Not with the mean and vulgar works of man,
> But with high objects, with eternal things,
> With life and Nature, purifying thus
> The elements of feeling and of thought,
> And sanctifying by such discipline
> Both pain and fear, until we recognize
> A grandeur in the beatings of the heart.
> (N p.4 ll.130-141)

In these lines nature and consciousness are linked, the individual before the fall and the individual after the fall, insofar as the formation of consciousness does not take place in a fall from nature, but in a process that cannot be envisaged without it. What happens to the boy in his childhood is that nature purifies and dedicates – fashions – his inner being in such a way that he who senses and what is sensed can no longer be distinguished. "Grandeur", which is found in the elevated natural phenomena, and which has marked the child, is found again as one elementary common rhythm in the body and the mind.

Great, pulsating nature – which we also meet in the first texts from 1798 ("an ebbing and a flowing mind") – is not a secure childhood garden of paradise, an earthly heaven. As in the early poems, life together with nature is also associated with pain and fear. When man, through the fearful and joyful meeting with sublime nature, experiences how the heart pounds and the mind rhythmically contracts and expands, this is thus also cosmic nature's meeting with itself.

The Sublime Pattern of Experience

The passage from *The Prelude*, 1799, thus expands the idea that the sublime experience – with its duality of pain and dizzy joy – receives its basic form in the child's early experience of nature. So the passage is an early statement of the main theme in *The Prelude*, 1799: grand, but also everyday nature as a formative element of the consciousness.

Life close to nature thus predisposes the child for the elevated, the Sublime – not only in tangible nature, but also in intangible, spiritual nature, which again are two sides of one and the same all-embracing phenomenon. For this reason it is important to maintain a distinction. For Wordsworth the Sublime is not identical with the experience of nature as such. On this point he seems to be in agreement with the foremost theoreticians on the Sublime: Burke and especially Kant and Schiller.[40] For all four of them, the Sublime points beyond the experience of physical nature to a regular pattern for human intellectual growth. This regularity is manifested in the elementary rhythm of expansion and contraction, where the boundaries of what is familiar and well-known are crossed; and this crossing, however frightening, eventually awakens joy because it is evidence of man's superior, innate intellectual powers, which are not subject to the compulsions of physical nature.

Here, however, the agreement between Wordsworth and particularly Kant comes to an end. For the isolation of the subjective and the resulting dualism between subject and object represented by Kant is not Wordsworth's position at this time. In Wordsworth's eyes it is not possible to view nature and consciousness as separate phenomena or concepts. For that reason the contemporary discussion as to whether the Sublime is present in the object – grand nature – or in the mind of the beholder (Kant's position) is based on wrong premises from a Wordsworthian perspective. At first sight, Wordsworth seems here to be in agreement with Schiller, who distinguishes between the Sublime in the object and the Sublime in the perceiving subject and thereby, in contrast to Kant, also ascribes Sublimity to external nature.

But Wordsworth takes a different direction from Schiller also and explains the relationship and the relative significance of external and internal nature. Thus he both claims the Sublime to be the token of a superior intellectual potential in man and at the same time maintains that this potential derives from the impression of grand external nature, and thereby he avoids subscribing to a dualistic point of view. According to the Wordsworth texts so far read, the individual sublime potential is formed in the meeting with grand cosmic nature – defined as the physical world infused by a universal consciousness ("one great mind" in *The Simplon Pass*, "spirit" in *Tintern Abbey*). In a way most characteristic of Wordsworth, the crucial factor in the experience of the Sublime is not the actual euphoric fear and blissful elevation, but the fact that the experience sinks down into the individual mind as a track or pattern. The original and immediate experience of fear and delight in the self turns out to have a lasting formative effect upon the nature of human consciousness in such a way as to enable man to expand his moral potential, not least by dint of being able to raise himself above the immediate sensuous experience of grand nature.

This meditative or reflective aspect of the experience of sublime nature does not necessarily result in a divorce of subject and object. In the eyes of Wordsworth, man can only rise above cosmic universal nature in his own imagination. While Kant, the greatest theorist of the Sublime, distinguishes between subject and object, consciousness and nature, Wordsworth's view is that such a distinction is false inevitably leading to intellectual self-delusion, for they are two sides of the same whole. Anyone not subject to such an illusion can achieve a profounder insight into nature – thanks to his life close to it in childhood.

The proper answer to the longing for a lost spontaneous and undivided – sublime – existence is not, however, to be found in a return to the lost natural surroundings or landscape of childhood. Wordsworth is already

aware of this in the boat poem, although at that stage he has no alternative to the provisional comfort of recalling the lost play of colours. The
alternative at which Wordsworth arrived during the two last years of the
century lay in a completely different direction – not in looking back, but
in the narrator's present – that is to say in the actual form of experience
and consciousness of the adult narrator, which nevertheless has its roots
in the boy's very earliest, intense communion with sublime nature – "from
his very dawn/Of infancy" (N p.3, ll.71-72).

Towards the end of the section about the beating heart, Wordsworth
expands this idea of the child's presence in the adult as a form or pattern
of experience, by describing the emergence of the creative and boundary-
crossing potential of the imagination. 44 lines were added in 1799 to the
original fragment (N pp.4-5, ll.142-185). In these Wordsworth presents two
related experiences which throw light on the sublime aspect in all its
wealth of contradiction – euphoria and melancholy, surrender and
reflection.

In the first there is a description of the noisy, skating boys' unhesitating
flight across the ice to the accompaniment of echoes in the ravines
blended with an alien, melancholy sound from the distant hills. Nature
replies in two ways, first as a perfect, familiar echo, and then in a way that
reveals its alien quality in relation to the boys' world.

Something similar occurs in the second version: complete unity – here
in the form of the movement – is broken, but this time not by nature. The
boy draws back from the others and cuts across the cosmic reflection of
a star (l.173), whereupon he experiences how the hills apparently of their
own volition continue their movement as he suddenly comes to a
standstill.

> – yet still the solitary cliffs
> Wheeled by me, even as if the earth had rolled
> With visible motion her diurnal round
> Behind me did they stretch in solemn train,
> Feebler and feebler, and I stood and watched
> Till all was tranquil as a summer sea.
> (N p.5, ll.180-185)

Separating himself more or less voluntarily from the spontaneous communion with the others and with nature, the boy simultaneously takes

part in an opposing, healing process, slightly reminiscent of the corresponding development in the boat poem. For both cosmic experiences of nature are dissolved by allowing the contours of the landscape to fade out in a manner reflecting a meditative state of rest – most clearly when his eye follows the landscape until it disappears, and everything becomes as motionless as a calm sea in summer.

These two episodes are followed up by the elaboration of the line from the original fragment: "A grandeur in the beatings of the heart", describing how this grandeur is implanted in the receptive child according to nature's plan. The powers of nature thus act with an intention which the adult narrator can read from the child's experiences while at the same time loyally retaining its animistic stance.

> Ye powers of earth, ye genii of the springs,
> And ye that have your voices in the clouds,
> And ye that are familiars of the lakes
> And of the standing pools, I may not think
> A vulgar hope was yours when ye employed
> Such ministry – when ye through many a year
> Thus, by the agency of boyish sports,
> On caves and trees, upon the woods and hills,
> Impressed upon all forms the characters
> Of danger or desire, and thus did make
> The surface of the universal earth
> With meanings of delight, of hope and fear,
> Work like a sea.[41]
> (N p.5-6 ll.186-198)

With the boy's games in nature as a medium, nature links elementary meanings, both repellent and attractive ("danger and desire") to its phenomena. In this state of tension we find the original formula for the Sublime. Partly its abundance of contrasts, partly the liberating climb leading to a reconciliation of the opposites. This is just what happens at the end of the quotation when the surface of the earth is in constant rhythmical movement like a faceted, living whole, similar to the ever-pulsating sea.[42] In this cosmic pulse we again find the ebb and flow metaphor from the early 1798 texts.

So for the child nature appears as a grand and manifold whole giving rise to diverse feelings of delight, hope and fear. And here too, it appears in such a way that it must not be seen merely as a projection on nature of the child's inner being. For it is rather the external which is projected into the child making consciousness and nature two sides of the same coin, quite simply because ever since the birth of the child they have been woven together – "interweave" is the word used in the first *Prelude* fragment.[43]

As the child's experience of nature is formed by that same nature, then delight and fear are not originally abstract concepts for purely inner, subjective feelings, but are ever associated with the concrete natural phenomena and experiences of nature that awaken these feelings in the child. Only when this interweaving is resolved – or better: seen through – can the abstract word arise and thus what we normally understand by language. In this sense "impressed" nature is a language before language, addressed to the child, and thereby a system of signs, by which the child conceives of itself as part of nature and not as an autonomous self.

So a child's way of understanding and experiencing can be dated to "the time of unrememberable being". At this stage the individual and the surrounding world are not yet conceived of as independent and separate in relation to each other, but as intimately linked – despite the fact that the original absolute presence has come to an end.

In other words, a significant change has come in relation to the young Wordsworth, who saw nature and consciousness as irrevocably distinct in the boat poem, where the sun disappears and can be brought back only by the action of the bard – and then for just a brief moment. This distinction between nature and consciousness is one important prerequisite for the purely metaphorical link between nature and human consciousness which Wordsworth created in both the 1787 and 1794 fragments, and which was only renounced when he wrote his way into a new view of nature in the course of 1798.

The "*Ah, not in vain*" passage from October-November 1798 has shown that the child's relationship to nature cannot be exhaustively described, either as a vegetative or conversely a subject-object relationship. For there is a question of a ceaseless and productive interaction in which the two elements are alternately active and passive, as has been seen in the first 198 lines of *The Prelude*, 1799 – and will be confirmed by what is to come. It is in this dialectic that the mind of the child and the very foundations of imagination take shape.[44]

The Starting-place of Being Fair

The remainder of the first part of the poem further develops this elementary dialectic, which can be summed up in the words: "the growth of mental power/And love of Nature's works" (N p.7 ll.257-258). The child's consciousness is nourished and formed during its very earliest years, just as the suckling is nourished at his mother's breast: "I held unconscious intercourse/With the eternal beauty/Drinking in/A pure organic pleasure" (N p.11 ll.394-396). Consciousness at this stage of development cannot be separated from nature as a physically, organic entity. Thus the key formulations of this relationship are "intertwine" (N p.4 l.130), "impressed my mind" (N p.8 l.283 and similar expressions p.6 l.194 and p.12 l.422), "implanted in my mind" (N p.9 l.334), "peopled (...)my mind" (N p.11 ll.377-378) and "Depicted on the brain" (N p.12 l.431). In one of the fragments from 1798 the expression "On my mind had stamped" is used (N p.489 l.125). This process of implantation and forming, which Wordsworth outlines for the first time in *The Pedlar* is nuanced and further extended in an intensive exploration of nature's impact on the content and the forms of consciousness. As it is put in a self-reflective passage: "Nor, sedulous as I have been to trace/How Nature by collateral interest,/And by extrinsic passion, peopled first/My mind with forms or beautiful or grand". (N p.11 ll.375-378)

The most important episode in this connection is the eight-year-old boy's confrontation with death when he witnesses a drowned man being pulled out of the river.

> I might advert
> To numerous accidents ... in flood or field,
> Quarry or moor, or 'mid the winter snows,
> Distresses and disasters, tragic facts
> Of rural history, that impressed my mind
> With images to which in following years
> Far other feelings were attached – with forms
> That yet exist with independent life,
> And, like their archetypes, know no decay.
> (N p.8 ll.279-287)

The line of thought is a clear extension of that in *The Pedlar*. The images and forms emotionally impressed on the mind acquire their own life and become indestructible.[45] This is why in direct continuation of the lines quoted, Wordsworth introduces the following section in this way:

> There are in our existence spots of time
> Which with distinct preeminence retain
> A fructifying virtue, whence, depressed
> By trivial occupations and the round
> Of ordinary intercourse, our minds –
> Especially the imaginative power –
> Are nourished and invisibly repaired;
> Such moments chiefly seem to have their date
> In our first childhood.
> (N p.8-9 ll.288-296)

Thanks to these imprinted, archetypal *spots of time*, consciousness can free itself from the trivialisation that normally occurs when event is added to event and everything becomes obvious and habitual. For in the imprinted images or forms the boundary-crossing, sublime dimensions of the first experience survive at least as a potential – not as content, but as structure. By keeping open access to such moments, such early childhood experiences, the imagination maintains its dynamic. Wordsworth expresses a similar idea in the second part of *The Prelude*, 1799, when he distinguishes between what is felt and how it is felt, and between content and form, allowing the latter to survive in the memory as potential: the expansive capacity of the intellect, the sense for the latently Sublime.

> ... that the soul –
> Remembering how she felt, but what she felt
> Remembering not – retains an obscure sense
> Of possible sublimity, to which
> With growing faculties she does aspire.
> (N p.23 ll.364-368)

The pre-conscious spots, which extend over all sense impressions and moods, have the same function. Wordsworth talks of them two sections further on in the first part of *The Prelude*, 1799, as something that maintains the child's intellectual organism. "All these were spectacles and sounds to which/I often would repair, and thence would drink/As at a fountain" (N p.10 ll.368-370), and "I held unconscious intercourse/With

74

the eternal beauty, drinking in/A pure organic pleasure from the lines/Of curling mist" (N p.11 ll.394-397). This is more than just a superficial metaphorical comparison with the organism's elementary taking of nourishment. For the condition Wordsworth depicts is precisely the condition beyond memory, in which consciousness is not freed from the body and the surrounding world. The suckling child does not conceive of itself as separate from its mother's body.[46] In immediate continuation of the *spots of time* quotation Wordsworth also talks of "The twilight of rememberable life" (l.298), which represents the same notion as the expression: "the time of unrememberable being", but the condition is placed a little further on in the development of the child on the threshold of individual memory.

But impressions exist from this "pre-conscious", non-reflective period other than those linked to turbulent or exciting events: states of elevated calm – not unlike the condition Wordsworth depicted in the boy's cosmic experience while skating:

> Those hallowed and pure motions of the sense
> Which seem in their simplicity to own
> An intellectual charm, that calm delight
> Which, if I err not, surely must belong
> To those first-born affinities that fit
> Our new existence to existing things
> And, in our dawn of being, constitute
> The bond of union betwixt life and joy.
> (N p.11 ll.383-390)

These emotional ties, which like an umbilical cord link life and joy together, are akin to the *spots of time*, although they are well hidden in the child's out-going, boisterous life as was the case in *Tintern Abbey*. Wordsworth compares these spots with "Gleams like the flashing of a shield" (N p.12 l.418). No conscious adaptation or acquisition of what nature communicates in such an extremely concentrated form takes place. Only later are the latent contents of these glimpses made manifest in recollection, and when that happens, the mind is elevated in the process.

> The earth
> And common face of Nature spake to me
> Remembrable things (...)

(...) doomed to sleep
Until maturer seasons called them forth
To impregnate and elevate the mind.
(N p.12 ll.418-426)

This is yet another description of the pattern of the sublime experience and its inextricable ties with the unconscious imprinting the child receives from nature. But the passage offers a new aspect which throws light on how it can be thought at all possible to put words to what is recalled from the pre-language state. Because the spots of time, these limited impressions, clearly precede the phase in life in which the child's ability to relate consciously to its own experiences is formed. The explanation is that the meditative process is not dependent on whether what is recalled was originally processed by the consciousness. The impression is there as an imprint existing in a torpid condition in the child until he has developed so far that the latent effect can manifest itself in consciousness and be formulated in language.

This meditative, retrospective experience is the adult's access to "the time of unrememberable being", because the self-oblivious retrospective ability is derived from the child's early, unreflective life in nature. The meditative contemplation of the adult connects with layers which have their roots in the unrememberable pre-linguistic stage where the border-line between inner and outer is not yet established. In this we find a plausible explanation of the decisive role which meditative cognition plays for Wordsworth.

In the quotation above, Wordsworth expands and re-formulates the presentation in *The Pedlar* of the involuntary reworking that occurs while the original impression survives. It is formed not as an act of the will, but as a process of filtration in the consciousness. Gradually, as other similar impressions accumulate, the impressed image is purged of the superficial and coincidental, so as only to be retained in its general characteristics – its "substantial lineaments" as Wordsworth puts it. These characteristics – which partly correspond to "pictured lines" in *The Pedlar* (l.92) – unite to form a kind of basic sketch working as a blue-print for the child's future sense impressions of similar phenomena (cf. the comparison found in *The Pedlar*). This basic sketch or type is, however, not only a familiar outline, a shade of colour, a pattern. As always with Wordsworth, the form is also more or less covertly linked with the emotional life:

76

> And thus
> By the impressive agency of fear,
> By pleasure and repeated happiness -
> So frequently repeated - and by force
> Of obscure feelings representative
> Of joys that were forgotten, these same scenes,
> So beauteous and majestic in themselves,
> Though yet the day was distant, did at length
> Become habitually dear, and all
> Their hues and forms were by invisible links
> Allied to the affections.[47]
> (N p.12-13 ll.432-442)

As already shown in connection with the early 1798 texts and the earlier episodes in *The Prelude*, the originally external natural phenomena or landscapes are associated with feelings.[48] As they are impressed on the consciousness the phenomenal colours and forms are linked to the entire gamut of feelings through constant repetition, so that outer and inner, form and content are dialectically bound together. The forms give rise to feelings, the feelings to forms.

The imaginative consequences of this association and internalisation Wordsworth examines for the first time in *The Pedlar* and subsequently formulates programmatically in *Tintern Abbey*. In *The Prelude*, 1799, these considerations are given a more down-to-earth and elementary form as Wordsworth turns back towards and into his own childhood, for instance when he joins natural phenomenon and intellectual or emotional reality together in the image of the beating heart - or when he rounds the first part off by synthesising the transformation of the emotionally charged shades of colour and forms into an imaginative spectacle. The concluding lines are quoted here, not from *The Prelude*, but from fragment *(f)* in the *JJ* manuscript, 1798. The first three, very important, lines of the fragment - emphasising that the foundation of the imagination is to be found in earliest childhood - are omitted in 1799.

> Those beauteous colours of my early years
> Which make the starting-place of being fair
> And worthy of the goal to which the(y) tend -
> Those recollected hours that have the charm
> Of visionary things, and lovely forms
> And sweet sensations, which throw back our life

And make our infancy a visible scene
On which the sun is shining.
(N p.493 ll.1-8)

The starting point is exactly the same as in the boat poem: the sensing of the wonderful colours that characterise the horizon of childhood experience and thereby a breakthrough of the meanings that are later separated out from phenomenal nature and formulated in words or concepts.

What in the old poem looked like a perfidious disappearance into the darkness, for which the bard defiantly had to compensate, is here balanced by the fact that the original impression provides the basis of the categories or forms in which the child and later the adult subsequently sees the world and himself, and which are expanded and expressed in constant repetition. The recall takes place each time as a process starting out from this deeply instilled, non-conceptual language of the senses ("those beauteous colours") – this pre-language consciousness ("the staring-place of being fair") which Wordsworth strived to approach in *The Ruined Cottage* and *Tintern Abbey*. From this first attempt Wordsworth goes on clarifying the idea of the creative potential encapsulated in the impression, eventually realising that the colours-and-feelings remembered as one entity are not a copy. But neither are they a purely arbitrary, subjective formation.

Inversion

Wordsworth therefore moves on to describe this pre-language potential for meaning in *The Prelude* as impressed and thus innate visual and emotional basic patterns which constitute the prerequisite for the formation of all subsequent meaning, and which therefore still affect the adult poet's language and imagery. So if these patterns are the basis of the imagination, this means that when they are stimulated they give visionary access to the unarticulated, early, unremembered forms, colours and feelings of childhood. In our adult lives we can thus experience the past as childhood arises as sun-drenched scenery before our inner, creative eye, the very organ of sight formed in our earliest childhood and now coming into action in the adult imagination: "a visible scene / On which the sun is shining."

The actual notion of the past being thrown back at us in the fragment *(f)* just quoted, plays on the experience occurring in the form of a sudden inversion. It can be viewed as a continuation of what looks more and more like an archetype in the earlier work: the turning back of the eyes in the boat poem and the image of the vibrant surface of the lake reflecting, throwing back the landscape in the 1794-fragment. In both cases an image is created in the form of a reflection or inversion. A natural phenomenon which exists or has existed, is at once mirrored and transformed. But the construction in 1798-1799 is used in a way strikingly different from the occccurrence in 1794. There is no longer any analogisation of nature and consciousness, but a process exclusively taking place within the realm of consciousness, or the imagination. The complex scenery reflected is imaginary, but in the specific sense that it was originally impressed or imprinted on the mind by nature. On this point there is complete agreement with the passage quoted above from the *JJ* manuscript.

The scenery originates in experiences with nature that now live on in the self as forms and feelings. They do not reproduce, the (re)create the scenery. It is indeed a "picture of the mind". The remarkable use of the word "throw" in the *JJ* quotation 1.6 thus refers to the fact both that we are the objects of powerful emotional forces releasing the vision and that the process takes the form of a leap out of normal consciousness. A radiant world which has hitherto been latently present beyond language is suddenly thrown into the customary adult world of language. Almost ten years after the bard of the boat poem sought to retain the same scene, the sunlight now announces itself in lines with an objective force of an entirely different kind, although just as in the boat poem it is seen as a purely mental phenomenon. The conception of the mental has changed – it is no longer a sphere sharply distinct from the world of phenomena, but dialectically tied to it. Consciousness is nature, nature consciousness. The faculty of vision set in motion in the process is, like the sun, of an objective intellectual kind: the kind of light – and thereby colour – which is implanted in us by nature in our childhood, and which is the light by which we actually see. Thus the term "unrememberable" does not simply characterize a prelinguistic world prior to any consciousness of the individual self, but the very forms impressed in the individual mind from its earliest being. These forms are now inherent in the adult consciousness and imagination. Consequently they cannot be separated from the workings of our mind including the act of remembering.

Between 1798 and 1799 Wordsworth came to the conclusion that this original sense of unity, this sense of the Sublime, had survived in the adult poet and was latently present in his way of sensing and remembering – and thus in his image-creating ability. That is to say as a visionary, formative spectacle, not as some kind of mental picture album. In this we find an essential reason why the young adult poet in the poems so far read is constantly preoccupied with the Sublime – and why the fundamental structures in the poems seem to be variations on one fundamental pattern of sublimity. During this period, the Sublime became for Wordsworth synonymous – not with specific subjects or forms of rhetoric – but with a pattern of experience, with physical and intellectual rhythms which released imprisoned poetical energies and opened up for new areas in the mind.

So for Wordsworth in 1798-1799, imagining is not creating something hitherto unseen, but discovering, seeing what already exists. Nature and consciousness are not distinct entities, but closely interrelated. The formative role of the imagination therefore is fused with its function as understanding or recognition. So *The Prelude* deals with (re-)discovering the sun behind the sun – with understanding external nature as the manifestational form for another nature. This other nature is not the Christian supra-nature, but the forgotten or hidden basic pattern for man's interpretative sensing of the world, which is imprinted in him in childhood and lives on in the adult poet's imagination – as unalterable powers, as the light in – and by – which he sees the world.

Two Consciousnesses
Wordsworth takes this principle with him into the second part of *The Prelude*, 1799, which is concerned with the same themes and insights. But the chronological framework is expanded both retrospectively and prospectively. Wordsworth proceeds beyond childhood and closes with the seventeen-year-old, but at the same time he looks even further back, right to the baby's symbiotic life with its mother – to the basis of "the time of unrememberable being".

This is presumably the reason why the second part is introduced by reflections both on Wordsworth's own position as narrator in relation to what is narrated and on the chasm that still seems to separate the person remembering from what is remembered:

> so wide appears
> The vacancy between me and those days,
> Which yet have such self-presence in my heart
> That sometimes when I think of them I seem
> Two consciousnesses – conscious of myself,
> And of some other being.
> (N p.14 ll.26-31)

Self-awareness, which according to its nature is dual (the consciousness thinks of itself), is furthermore enclosed in a duality. The adult, self-aware narrator does not simply relate to himself, but also to the self he once was – in the same way as he does in *Tintern Abbey*. The person for whom childhood is a sun-drenched landscape thus experiences an intense presence in his heart. But in the longer run this visionary presence awakens the consciousness of absence, an unsurmountable distance: the former self appears as a quite different being. And it is this paradoxical relationship between two consciousnesses in the narrator, this experience of being non-contemporary with himself that Wordsworth seeks to come to understand by once more asking himself how he has become what he is now: an individual whose consciousness of himself *as* an individual is closely tied to the presence of another, earlier self.

So the second part starts with a description of how the child's un-reflected, outgoing and yet egocentric behaviour undergoes a transformation born of a growing need for a more subdued, observant attitude, "calmer pleasures" (N p.15 l.49):

> And the vainglory of superior skill
> Were interfused with objects which subdued
> And tempered them, and gradually produced
> A quiet independence of the heart.
> (N p.15 ll.69-72)

In other words an internalisation takes place in relation to nature, an event signifying a move to make the heart independent – the ability to sense and feel that is in general the individual's growth centre. The heart thus also becomes the organ for a meditative examination of its own functions and thus acquires the same relationship to nature, the world of the senses, as the other or inner eye.

At such a moment when meditating on nature, the fourteen-year-old boy anticipates a later age's contemplative relationship with nature and breaks with his habits so far – "a momentary trance/That far outran the habit of my mind" (N p.18 ll.178-179):

> Fair scenes – that dying I would think on you,
> My soul would send a longing look to you,
> Even as the setting sun, while all the vale
> Could nowhere catch one faint memorial gleam,
> Yet with the last remains of his last light
> Still lingered, and a farewell lustre threw
> On the dear mountain-tops where first he rose.
> (N p.18 ll.168-174)

The passage is a further elaboration on the section quoted earlier from *The Vale of Esthwaite*, 1789. Wordsworth has retained its gradual transition from sun to soul, from the rhythm of nature to the rhythm of intellect. This almost imperceptible fusion of nature and consciousness belongs to the same meditative, calm state described in the early 1798 texts and Part One of *The Prelude*, 1799. Even there it is associated with the Sublime. Indeed, properly speaking, this receptiveness – anticipated in the vibrating surface of the lake and in the human mind – is the most elevated form possible for the sublime experience, compared with the child's spontaneous, passionate crossing of boundaries. Wordsworth sums up his description of the process of internalisation in a simple portrayal of the sublimity of mental calm, recalling fragment *i* from the *Alfoxden* notebook, quoted above, in which the light from the moon sinks into his heart:

>   the calm
> And dead still water lay upon my mind
> Even with the weight of pleasure, and the sky,
> Never before so beautiful, sank down
> Into my heart and held me like a dream.
> (N p.19 ll.210-214)

As in the corresponding charged depictions of the soul and the landscape in the early work, the same – in the true sense of the word – elementary images are found again. The water with the reflecting surface, the sky or the landscape reflected, the observing self caught in the dialectic between the two. But there is not as in 1794 a question of the mind being *like* the lake. The static quality of the analogy is replaced by a dynamism in the metaphor. This manifests itself as a reduplication of the actual mirror function, and this again forms itself as a metaphorical gradual transition from the physical to the spiritual – a metamorphosis. The surface of the water with its mirror rests on the mind, which is delighted by its weight. The mind, which in the contemplation of the shining water has itself become a receptive, reflecting surface, receives the sinking sky.[49] But the objective of the movement downwards is not the surface of the mind. It goes beyond this. The sky sinks down, permeates the reflective surface and settles in the innermost region, in the heart, where it lives on as a dream-like state of consciousness.[50]

In this meditative absorption, the sky is seemingly drawn down to the earth. But the union of the heavenly and the earthly does not take place by way of the self's own power, as when the boy in Part One clambers up, hanging out above the raven's nest, becomes one with the heavens. Here it is the water and the sky, nature that actively forces its way into the mind and dissolves the normal boundaries between outer and inner. The child's outgoing, expansive sensing experience is replaced by a passive meditative state of consciousness. An analogous form of meditative transition can be found in the ending of the skating episode, where the dissolution of the contours of sensuous nature makes way for an experience of nature's sublime, unbounded dimensions. Both experiences reveal how, behind the boy's passionate physical exertion in the face of nature, there exists another and deeper potential for achievement linked to reflection, but expressly understood as the meditative, non-analytical mutual relationship which mirroring is. This kind of reflection or mirroring contains an objectivity that again builds on the fundamental similarity between consciousness and nature. Reflection in this sense thus represents a receptiveness and a symmetry or reversibility in man's relationship with nature, which implies that the person seeing and the object seen can fuse into a third, common element.

This idea in Wordsworth does not only throw light on the concept of the Sublime in these writings, but also on the conceptual history of the Sublime. As is well known, the sphere of the Sublime – in the modern reception of the old concept – is extended at the end of the 18th century to encompass inner, human nature. Wordsworth takes this process a decisive step further around 1798-1799, partly by maintaining the existence of a cosmic, sublime nature and seeing the sublime potential of the human mind as the valid product of this nature, and partly by implanting a development into man's way of seeing the Sublime, extending from the impression made on the mind by grand nature to the effect of that nature on the mind, which produces cosmic visions. Wordsworth thereby makes superfluous all discussion as to whether the Sublime is to be found within or without. It is present in both. The sublime dialectic between inner and outer is crucial to the development of the human mind.

That False Secondary Power

An important new stage is reached as the child matures and nature ceases to be merely a medium or a means and becomes an end in itself. The umbilical cord is cut:

> Those incidental charms which first attached
> My heart to rural objects, day by day
> Grew weaker, and I hasten on to tell
> How Nature, intervenient till this time
> And secondary, now at length was sought
> For her own sake. But who shall parcel out
> His intellect by geometric rules
> Split like a province into round and square?
> Who knows the individual hour in which
> His habits were first sown even as a seed?
> Who shall point as with a wand, and say
> 'This portion of the river of my mind
> Came from yon fountain'[51]
> (N p.19-20 ll.237-249)

This presentation of the way in which the boy breaks out of his close relationship with a maternal nature is the starting point for a polemic against the potential for intellectual reflection appearing at the very time when the boy is maturing and freeing himself from nature. Wordsworth rejects the possibility of turning the genesis of the intellect into the object of abstract analysis, and in direct continuation of the passage above – in words addressed to his friend Coleridge – he characterises intellectual, abstract reflection as false:

> Thou my friend, art one
> More deeply read in thy own thoughts, no slave
> Of that false secondary power by which
> In weakness we create distinctions, then
> Believe our puny boundaries are things
> Which we perceive, and not which we have made.
> (N p.20 ll.249-254)

From a philosophical point of view, this is a key passage in *The Prelude*, 1799, but it is also found in a fragment in the manuscript *Peter Bell MS 2*, presumably from February 1799 – that is to say from the period when the fragments to Part One of *The Prelude* were being worked together and built up into the whole we know. The fragment is not adopted in its entirety in *The Prelude*, 1799. The lines omitted, originally forming a frame round those incorporated, will be quoted below, for they are important for an understanding of the position from which Wordsworth speaks in the Part Two of *The Prelude*, 1799. (That part of the fragment which was transferred to *The Prelude*, 1799, is printed below in italics).

The fragment begins with an expression of intellectual scepticism towards normal consciousness. The forms and images that float around in our consciousness do not represent our true being. Normal consciousness must be considered as secondary – a fall out of and away from the primary consciousness[52] of the inner life that is in all things:

> I seemed to learn
> That what we see of forms and images
> Which float along our minds, and what we feel
> Of active or recognizable thought,
> Prospectiveness, or intellect or will,
> Not only is not worthy to be deemed
> Our being, to be prized as what we are,
> But is the very littleness of life.
> Such consciousness I deem but accidents,

Relapses from that one interior life
That lives in all things, sacred for the touch
Of *that false secondary power by which*
In weakness we create distinctions, then
Believe our puny boundaries are things
Which we perceive, and not which we have made -
In which all beings live with God, themselves
Are God, existing in one mighty whole,
As undistinguishable as the cloudless east
At noon is from the cloudless west, when all
The hemisphere is one cerulian blue.[53]
(N p.496)

Wordsworth is striking out at the secondary intellectual ability which in its attempt to classify and analyse has separated itself from its object, making the mistake of taking its own concepts for the matter itself. In that sense it does not reflect, as does the meditative form of experience, but projects itself. With its conceptual apparatus it excludes a priori the possibility of entering into a cognitive relationship to its object, for it only sees the classifications it has created. As quoted previously from *The Tables Turned:* "Our meddling intellect/Mis-shapes the beauteous forms of things/ - We murder to dissect". (PW IV p.57)

As has been seen, the link with childhood is not established by way of an intellectual conceptual reconstruction, but in a visionary leap, in a throw-back vision of the sun-drenched landscape of childhood. So in Wordsworth reflection means two widely different things: On the one hand an intellectual pursuit, abstracting and dissecting, in which the concepts get in the way of true insight. On the other hand a meditative form of experience characterised by being reflective, i.e. mirroring, receptive and at the same time visionary, re-generative, non-differentiating and thereby committed to existing concrete, physical or psychological reality.

As for the latter meaning of the word reflective, Wordsworth alludes not only to the introspective powers of his dear friend but also to an old and widespread Christian hermeneutic tradition of linking spiritual meaning to the phenomena of the world of the senses, which are thus given dual significance, as is the case in the book of nature tradition.[54] In addition to their customary phenomenally rooted meaning, phenomena conceal a second, deeper, real meaning. And this meaning does not concern relationships of cause and effect, but essence, true identity.

What falsifies the abstractive ability to reflect and differentiate is, then, that it denies the primary, i.e. ever-present sublime whole in which no boundary between outer and inner exists, but everything is one radiant blue heaven as in the quotation above. This vision of the actual cosmic state – which we have met in two versions in *The Prelude*, 1799 – at the same time dissolves the traditional Christian distinction between God as Creator and Man as Creation. To Wordsworth there is no original supra-nature beyond physical nature, but only one nature encompassing every-thing, including the spiritual dimension. In looking to the Christian hermeneutic tradition, Wordsworth changes it fundamentally.

On these premises in Part Two of *The Prelude*, 1799, Wordsworth rejects all talk of a first beginning as a logical impossibility dependent on a confusion of incompatible categories: the visionary category of nature meditation and the externally classifying category of the intellect:

> Hard task to analyse a soul, in which
> Not only general habits and desires,
> But each most obvious and particular thought -
> Not in a mystical and idle sense,
> But in the words of reason deeply weighed -
> Hath no beginning.
> (N p.20 ll.262-267)

Wordsworth does not reject the actual possibility of speaking of the child and its "progress" in its state before becoming conscious of itself, i.e. becoming an individuality. This possibility is not only theoretically present in his view of nature as a series of stages of forms and potentials; it is also realised in *The Prelude*'s own visionary memory project which looks back to "the time of unrememberable being" and "the starting place of being fair".

On the other hand Wordsworth rejects any possibility that the adult, analytical faculty can reach back to an absolute starting point by way of reflection. Individuality is a late formation in the development of the individual, and its starting point is beyond the reach of the intellect, which comes into being only long after the child's unrememberable pre-language world.[55] The intellect cannot penetrate behind itself. So every conceptual attempt to discover a first beginning is illusory.

But this is not to say that the period before memory cannot be portrayed. For what applies to analysis does not apply to the ability to meditate and imagine. As he states in Part Two of *The Prelude*, 1799, Wordsworth is not interested in what was felt, but how it was felt, not in the concrete, datable, authentic chronology, but in the typical pattern of experience inherent in the actual occurrence, subsequently impressed on the mind. In immediate continuation of the quotation Wordsworth depicts the infant's life with its mother in the non-individual, pre-language phase which is the beginning of every human life. In doing so Wordsworth is not attempting to reconstruct the absolute beginning of his individual being. He is simply presenting us with the adult poet's vision of the pre-individual phase of the archetypal developmental process: "Blessed the infant babe – / For my best conjectures I would trace/The progress of our being". (267-269)

So the insight at which Wordsworth arrives in the course of 1798-1799 can be summed up by saying that the forms or patterns of experience from this early phase constitute the essential core of the sublime experience of unity – and furthermore that these forms make the adult poet's vision possible. As has already been seen many times in the preceding sections, the adult mind contains deep layers of impressions, unremembered traces and forms, which can be activated via the meditative, visionary activities of the imagination. It is in relation to this non-discursive subject that the intellect is considered secondary and treacherous. I would therefore maintain that Wordsworth's memory concept, at least in this early form, is driven by an imperative need to explore the Sublime and discover its genealogy, not as a philosophical or aesthetic concept, but as a basic form of consciousness deriving from life as experienced not from abstract speculation.

Wordsworth's description of how the infant's life with its mother is formative for all its subsequent life must be read in this light. Her tender eyes sow the seeds of what later will become the child's soul, its intellectual identity:

```
              - blest the babe
        Nursed in his mother's arms, the babe who sleeps
        Upon his mother's breast, who, when his soul
        Claims manifest kindred with an earthly soul,
        Doth gather passion from his mother's eye.
        Such feelings pass into torpid life
        Like an awakening breeze, and hence his mind,
        Even in the first trial of its powers,
        Is prompt and watchful, eager to combine
        In one appearance all the elements
        And parts of the same object, else detached
        And loth to coalesce.
        (N p.20 ll.269-280)
```

A breeze, a breath of air – a breath – awakens the child from its first vegetative dormancy to a purely physical, intimate, pre-language dialogue with the mother, centred on the meeting of the eyes and the beating of hearts – "I held mute dialogues with my mother's heart" (N p.21, l.313). The image focuses on the natural power that awakens, forms and maintains the feelings relating the child to all around it. In one of the fragments for *The Prelude*, 1799, there is a description of the actual cosmic power literally inspiring the child:

```
              - oh bounteous power,
        In childhood, in rememberable days,
        How often did thy love renew for me
        Those naked feelings which when thou wouldst form
        A living thing thou sendest like a breeze
        Into its infant being.
        (N p.489 ll.109-114)
```

The subject in this creative act is the mother. So the basic notion in *The Prelude* of the unity of all things and love as the unifying force – which also figures in the *Peter Bell* fragment – has its root in the mother's all-embracing, loving closeness to the infant:

```
        Along his infant veins are interfused
        The gravitation and the filial bond
        Of Nature that connect him with the world.
        (N p.21, ll.292-294)
```

The small boy's relationship with the world being thus literally incorporated is not only passively receptive, but active as well:

>   – his mind,
> Even as an agent of the one great mind,
> Creates, creator and receiver both,
> Working but in alliance with the works
> Which it beholds. Such, verily, is the first
> Poetic spirit of our human life –
> (N p.21 ll.301-305)

This dialectic between receiving and creating in the child's relationship to
nature is an important premise for Wordsworth's conception of the
imagination. Indeed, it could be maintained that imagination acquiring
such a crucial role for Wordsworth is the consequence of the original
sublime dialectic between the child and the mother surviving in imagination as the fundamental correlation between the self and universal nature.

As a consequence, *The Prelude*, 1799 also states something distinctly new
about the imagination – and about the actual sublime experience which
is its essence or basic structure. This is that the two have common ground
in the child's relationship – not to nature in a broad, unspecific sense, but
to the mother, who initiates the child to nature or who quite simply *is*
nature – the earliest form in which universal nature presents itself to the
child.

> In one beloved presence (...)
> (...) there exists
> A virtue which irradiates and exalts
> All objects through all intercourse of sense.
> (N p.21 ll.285 and 288-290)

The loving presence of the mother incarnates the cosmic informative,
uplifting, sublime power expressing itself in all phenomena, "the one great
mind". This power, then, does not only reveal itself to the child in the
phenomena of the sensuous world as such, but in the very earliest
interchange between the sensing and the sensed ("all intercourse of
sense"): love between mother and child.

An Obscure Sense of Possible Sublimity

A break occurs at this point in the second part of *The Prelude*, 1799. The boy is deserted – the mother dies, an autobiographical fact which does not, however, preclude the possibility that this death can also at the same time be seen in a more general light as the inevitable breaking up of the primal close relationship.[56] However, the formation of the boy's being and senses that has taken place survives as a structure in his consciousness – "the building stood, as if sustained/By its own spirit". (N p.22 ll.352-353) This continuity Wordsworth portrays in the remainder of the poem, which takes the form of a panorama of the boy's development until the age of 17. In his predisposition to the Sublime the "universal power" (N p.23 l.374) and the self's own imprinted potential converge. Once implanted in the elementary physical life close to his mother – (cf. "I held mute dialogues with my mother's heart") – a sense for the grand relationships and diversity of nature lives on, becoming the source of elevated feelings – "sublimer joy" (N p.22 l.351), "elevated mood" (N p.223 l.355) – and consequently of the image-creating, visionary talent which he quite literally drinks in with his mother's milk: "Thence did I drink the visionary power". (N p.23 l.360)

This ability then is not only a result of the formation of the mind, but also of a breaking away from what originally awakens the elevated moods, first the mother, and later all the experiences and phenomena that are recited in *The Prelude*, 1799. What is left stands as a dynamic spiritual structure, destined to transcend the limitations of normal senses and normal consciousness:

> the soul –
> Remembering how she felt, but what she felt
> Remembering not – retains an obscure sense
> Of possible sublimity, to which
> With growing faculties she doth aspire.
> (N p.23 ll.364-368)

The sense of the Sublime having become obscure is due to the original sublime presence no longer being physically there. The intuiting longing betokens an original, now vanished, sublimity which has received its fundamental form in the relationship with the mother. Sublimity is, however, not permanently centred on her in Wordsworth. The delight in experiencing the Sublime is certainly the delight of re-experiencing, but it is not a regression with the impossible aim of being re-united with what is definitively lost. As we have observed, the sublime expansion in the self presupposes a detachment from the origins. This detachment makes way for an understanding of the supra-individual, cosmic dimensions which the individual first encountered in the form of the mother, though without being aware of them. Now they are no longer limited to her person.

So there is an inversion of the individual ties to his past while at the same time the limits of individuality are transcended – in much the same way as, but more clearly than, in *Tintern Abbey*. In the fragment quoted above from the *JJ* manuscript: "sweet sensations, which throw back our life" the life of the past is thrown back into the present self. The fragment describes the actual moment at which the image is formed in the visionary imagination and thus in the poem. This is quite explicitly not a compensatory act. For the formation of the image is caused by the awakening of a sense originally created by nature but overlooked by the intellect.

This confirms yet again that the sublime experience cannot be interpreted as a simple projection of the self's longing. On the contrary it is a manifestation of a truly existing universal power which fashioned the child in its image, but has since been forgotten or discarded. So to Wordsworth it is not longing that disposes the self to the Sublime, but conversely the experience of the Sublime that has originally left traces in the mind subsequently making the self long for the grand both without and within itself.

> And not alone
> In grandeur and in tumult, but no less
> In tranquil scenes, that universal power
> And fitness in the latent qualities
> And essence of things, by which the mind
> Is moved with feelings of delight, to me
> Came strengthened with a superadded soul,
> A virtue not its own.
> (N p.23 ll.371-378)

This correspondence between the individual form of consciousness and cosmic nature is created in, but not identical with, the relationship between child and mother, which can thus be viewed as the earliest, but not the last or the sole, manifestation of the cosmic.

This, however, does not mean that the attraction to seek the past does not exist. It certainly does. But Wordsworth is aware of it, that is to say he interprets it. We must therefore not confuse the position of the narrator with that of the child or the youth.

For the person who, like the boy in *The Prelude*, has begun to divorce himself from the immediate intercourse with nature, the sublime experience changes dramatically. It is now something that to an increasing extent must be sought and which therefore tends, simultaneously to escape the seeker. It is no longer a total, all-embracing condition, but parcelled out in *spots of time*, pregnant, cherished moments of intense presence. The experience of the Sublime thus develops in a dialectic between two sets of opposites: on the one hand the temporal contrast between the pregnant moments and the states in between that provide a negative definition of the Sublime; and on the other the contrast between light and darkness, up and down, delight and fear, which characterises the actual physical or psychological process leading to the sublime experience.

In the light of the presence of the Sublime in the relationship between mother and child, this dialectic, however, must also be interpreted as a tension between looking back and looking forward. Within the framework of *The Prelude*, 1799, this tension is mainly expressed indirectly in the disquiet at separation from the mother, which is at once both enforced and willed. We have observed it in the boy's confrontations with a threatening nature far from what is familiar and safe – for instance in the episode in the boat or the dead man, in the boy's conquest of gravity in the raven's nest episode and in the skater's suspension of time.

In his poetry about the Sublime in 1798-1799, Wordsworth then exploits the very energies that are liberated in the suspension or rather change of direction of the powerful, regressive drives.

An Auxiliar Light

The creative and lucid spiritual power that reveals itself in the child is no more the result of reflection in an intellectual sense than is its effect in the adult poet. But this all changes in the final part of *The Prelude*, represented by just under 150 lines in all. As he grows older, the boy becomes aware

93

of his own abilities. At the same time the narrator moves into the foreground establishing his position in relation to the youth, who by now is seventeen years old. This last phase is introduced with an almost parallel version of the lines quoted earlier, ll.210-214, in which the heavens sink down into the boy's heart:

> Oft in those moments such a holy calm
> Did overspread my soul that I forgot
> The agency of sight, and what I saw
> Appeared like something in myself, a dream,
> A prospect in my mind.
> (N p.24 ll.397-401)

The meditative state of sacred peace – as we have seen before – is transformed into an interior image from which the surrounding world disappears. But the description is here extended to include the next stage of the process of the imagination. In place of the external world an inner world emerges, and what the boy sees is manifested as a landscape (painting), "A prospect in my mind". This inner dreamlike world has taken over the structure of the world of the senses. So, in "forgetting" how to use the sense of sight, the poet explicitly does not stop perceiving but aquires a new power of seeing.

This spontaneous inner, formative power ("plastic power", l.411) lives on in the young man, where it develops further and finally becomes conscious. The inner eye itself turns into a light shining out from within actively encompassing the world of phenomena. In contrast to the original text, this sun even shines its light on the sinking physical sun. Arndt's sun is infinitely far away.

> An auxiliar light
> Came from my mind, which on the setting sun
> Bestowed new splendour; the melodious birds,
> The gentle breezes, fountains that ran on
> ... Obeyed
> A like dominion ...
> (N p.24 ll.417-422)

This self-aware, out-going visionary power makes the young man see relationships where the normal consciousness finds none – "affinities/In objects where no brotherhood exists/To common minds" (N p.25 l.433-435). And as for the child, everything combines in his consciousness to form a cosmic ocean: "I at this time/Saw blessings spread around me like a sea" (ibid. l.443-444) and a single life: "I saw one life, and felt that it was joy" (ibid. l.460). The seeing implicit here in the verb "saw" is not that of the physical eye, but that of the heart, which is able to transcend the immediate phenomenal manifestations:

> I felt the sentiment of being spread
> O'er all that moves, and all that seemeth still,
> O'er all that, lost beyond the reach of thought
> And human knowledge, to the human eye
> Invisible, yet liveth to the heart ...
> (N p.25 ll.450-454)

Wordsworth maintains that such insight into real being cannot be achieved on the basis of the secondary intellectual abilities which the adult normally relies on. Only the sense that is linked to the heart, but which normal consciousness knows nothing of, is sufficient. This is the heart which ever since the baby's silent dialogue with the mother's heart has beaten in time with grand nature, the universe, and whose rhythm now holds *The Prelude* together.

Seen through the eyes of the experienced narrator, and with the wisdom of hindsight, the price for the self-aware manner in which the young man conceives of the world and confidently ascribes to it qualities – which it does not immediately possess – is an untenable innocence, an unconscious refusal to let go of the maternal nature which assumed the role of the biological mother. The young man is on his way into a phase in life that will disappoint him and repudiate his boyish expectation of the cohesion of all things.

This crisis has already been touched on in *The Pedlar*, where it expressly depends on the young man's will to look the sombre, destructive forces of nature in the eye.[57]

> Nature was at his heart, and he perceived
> Though yet he knew not how, a wasting power
> In all things which from her sweet influence
> Might tend to wean him, therefore with her hues
> Her forms and with the spirit of her forms

He clothed the nakedness of austere truth.
(PW V p.384 ll.202-207)

As the boy grows older, the inner pressure becomes too great and breaks out in the twenty-year-old as mental disturbance:

But now, before his twentieth year was pass'd
Accumulated feelings press'd his heart
With an increasing weight; he was overpower'd
By Nature, and his mind became disturbed.
(PW V p.384 ll. 221-224)

The following description of the young man's feverish and indissoluble ties with nature transferred, with some changes, to *The Prelude*, 1799, where it forms part of the portrait of the seventeen-year-old towards the end of Part Two, but now told in the first person. The passage "for in all things/I saw one life, and felt that it was joy" is thus – with a change of the personal pronoun from third to first person singular – lifted from *The Pedlar* (PW V p.385 ll.251-252)

This crisis is meanwhile much toned down in *The Prelude*. Here it rather seems to be a matter of the young man's meeting the world with a consciousness that is incommensurable with an adult way of experiencing. Therefore, the last extreme childish manifestations in the exaltation of the seventeen-year-old are the subject of gentle irony on the part of the narrator. He can neither condemn nor reject, for the light the young man adds to the sun – like the bard in the boat poem – is not a mere illusion, because in the youthful subjectivism the child's genuine, egocentric way of experiencing lives on.

The young seventeen-year-old, then, finds himself at an intermediate stage between child and adult. His view of the world is not sufficient for the narrator in the process of remembering, but nevertheless it constitutes the indispensable link back to another form of consciousness, a link that is of crucial moral significance for the adult at the time of writing.

– if, in this time
Of dereliction and dismay, I yet
Despair not of our nature, but retain
A more than Roman confidence, a faith
That fails not, in all sorrow my support,

The blessing of my life, the gift is yours
Ye mountains, thine O Nature. Thou hast fed
My lofty speculations, and in thee
For this uneasy heart of ours I find
A never-failing principle of joy
And purest passion.
(N p.26 ll.486-496)

In this context it is possible to read all the 1798-1799 texts quoted above as important stages in a grandiose attempt to retain the links with the lost world without letting go of what is, and without losing oneself in what was.

There was a Boy
This link consisted of more than mere chance, individual glimpses of memory – a fact to which Wordsworth began to realise in earnest between 1798 and 1799. On the last few pages we have traced the development of Wordsworth's view of the relationship between nature and consciousness. Looking back, the main stages in this process can be considered a further development and in part a re-interpretation of the boat poem's basic three-phased experience of the world, as illustrated in the simple diagram below. First there is the totality of radiant, immediately sensed colours (1), then the move towards the dark (2) and finally the mediative attempt to return and re-establish the lost, colourful unity, though now within the poet's inner being (3).

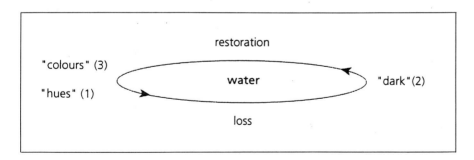

The re-establishment of what has been lost takes the form of a provisional suspension of time and space through the imagination. This suspension of the fall motivates the artistic use of the original, spontaneous sublime experience as the formative agent.

The symmetrical structure of the boat poem is not limited to this one poem, but is a repeated pattern, form and content in one, inextricably linked to Wordsworth's concept of the Sublime. This pattern implies an inverse movement corresponding to the one seen in some of the texts above as reduplication, mirroring, throwing back. In the boat poem the inversion consists in the darkness-seeking involuntary movement – associated with time in its merciless progress – being reversed and subsequently returned to its starting point – light and radiant colours, but on an explicitly reflective, aesthetic level. In this Wordsworth seems to be in keeping with the quotation from Hölderlin. All this is undertaken in a horizontal circular movement, respecting the axis of light and dark constituted by the reflective surface of the water. This nostalgic time-dissolving structure is decisively changed around 1798-1799.

The transformation is prepared as far back as the fragment from *An Evening Walk*, 1794, in which Wordsworth uses the water's reflective quality in quite a different way from what he did in the boat poem. Whereas in the boat poem the water reflects the loss – the division into light and inevitable darkness – in distinct, successive sense perceptions, the water in *An Evening Walk* reflects the landscape as a cosmic unity in a single visual impression which suspends the differences in space and time. In the reflected landscape or sky, what was and what is are united in a dual image. As a consequence the dynamic structure no longer unfolds horizontally and definitively, but vertically and dialectically as a sinking movement and a subsequent reflective throwing back of what has been sunk, while the surface of the water is retained as a horizontal axis.

Mirroring or the symmetrical inversion and its connection with Wordsworth's view of nature and the Sublime about 1798-1799, is given its most concentrated and refined expression in the poem *There was a boy*.

This poem exists in three versions: as a fragment from October-November 1798 in which only the first two stanzas of the final poem is included. Then a version containing a number of major and minor changes, the most important of which is the addition of a verse. This version was included in the second edition of *Lyrical Ballads*, 1800. Finally, this version appears as part of Book Fifth of *The Prelude*, 1805, though with a small number of changes from the 1800 version. This version is quoted below the original fragment in the notes.[58]

> There was a boy – ye knew him well, ye cliffs
> And islands of Winander – many a time
> At evening when the stars had just begun
> To move along the edges of the hills,
> Rising or setting, would he stand alone
> Beneath the trees or by the glimmering lake,
> And there with fingers interwoven, both hands
> Pressed closely palm to palm, and to his mouth
> Uplifted, he as through an instrument
> Blew mimic hootings to the silent owls,
> That they might answer him. And they would shout
> Across the wat'ry vale, and shout again,
> Responsive to his call, with quivering peals
> And long halloos, and screams, and echoes loud,
> Redoubled and redoubled – concourse wild
> Of mirth and jocund din. And when it chanced
> That pauses of deep silence mocked his skill,
> Then sometimes in that silence, while he hung
> Listening, a gentle shock of mild surprize
> Has carried far into his heart the voice
> Of mountain torrents; or the visible scene
> Would enter unawares into his mind
> With all its solemn imagery, its rocks,
> Its woods, and that uncertain heaven, received
> Into the bosom of the steady lake.
> (N p.172 and 174 ll.389-422)

For reasons unknown the fragment was not incorporated into *The Prelude*, 1799. The change from third to first person singular has by many interpreters been used as an argument in support of an autobiographical interpretation of the fragment, even though the two later versions retain the third person.[59] I shall attempt to show that this change might be explained in a different way.

The poem is about a boy's life close to nature, made concrete in his imitation of the hooting of the owls and their – or the echo's – reply in a jubilant chaos of unarticulated noise. He is reminiscent of the young hunter in *The Prelude*, also in that nature mocks his self-assured behaviour by not always giving him the answer expected.[60] The profound quiet opens up for another sense experience, not self-occasioned and the voice not only of nature, but also of its grand elements – those we already know as the regular inventory of the Sublime: the rocks, the woods, the sky, the water of the lake.

If we look a little more closely at the details of the last lines of the final version, the well-known meditative pattern appears, but in a far more complex form than hitherto. The lines do not only describe how nature sinks down into the mind. This movement is repeated – mirrored – in the very image entering the mind of the boy: the image of the landscape being "received / Into the bosom of the steady lake". These final lines fall into two stages. In the first stage the audible natural scenery – the voices of the mountain streams – is carried deep into the boy's heart. In the second, it is the visible natural scenery entering into his mind. Together, the two sense impressions describe the child's unreflective and in that sense passive acceptance of the impulses of nature – the imprints which in *The Prelude* are referred to by verbs such as impress or depict. But in addition the two stages in the movement from heart to mind also suggest a movement within the boy towards the threshold of a more reflective attitude because the passage is even more complicated. As we have already noted, a sinking movement and a corresponding reception of the imagery of nature takes place within the second stage: the calm lake – the calm water – embracing the surrounding landscape with the wooded rocks and the sky, that is to say reflecting it on its bright surface.[61] The "visible scene" is elaborated as a landscape in a poetical or painterly sense, i.e. a number of elements of nature composed to form a whole, (cf. the expression "prospect" clearly alluding to the composition of a landscape painting). This whole has apparently been imprinted into the boy by nature. However, it is not he who reproduces it and calls it a prospect, for he receives the impression passively and unknowingly.

Who is it, then, actively reproducing as a landscape the sense impressions which were originally received unconsciously? It is the very same adult narrator who in 1798 could not decide whether to use "he" or "I" of the boy. Irrespective of any external circumstances to which this indecision could be attributed, it can be related to the fact, based on the innate logic of the text, that the narrator is detached from the child's unreflecting relationship to nature and therefore uncertain whether he should or has the power to bridge the gap between the child and himself.

It is this gap which is called "the vacancy between me and those years" in *The Prelude*, 1799. The uncertainty is not removed until later in the final, extended version of the poem.

The narrator's picture of the landscape is thus formed by a consciousness that in its contemplation and suggested superior knowledge is divorced from the child's experience of nature, but which at the same time has visionary access to the child's realm of experience. This is supported by the fact that the image of the lake receiving the surrounding nature on its surface is also an image of the unreflective receptive mind of the boy – in the reflective adult poet's mind. Thus he can observe what the child only experiences unconsciously: the gradual moving away from his original inarticulate relationship to nature – the state which in *Tintern Abbey* is designated by the word "appetite" – and into the fragile start of another, meditative preoccupation with nature. This process of transformation corresponds to the swallowing up of the animal element which *The Pedlar* speaks of in the lines quoted above: "Sensation, soul and form/All melted into him. They swallowed up/His animal being".

In *There was a boy,* this incipient transformation of the boy's consciousness is illustrated by the sinking movement and the fact that the landscape is dual, mirrored as illustrated in the symmetrical triangles in the following diagram shown on page 102.

However, this duality in *There was a boy* is itself subjected to a dual point of view. What the boy experiences as a sublime, cosmic whole contains for the adult narrator the seeds of its own termination within it. The immediate situation (the top triangle in the diagram) is replaced by its meditative reflection (the lower, mirrored triangle in the diagram). This duality is another expression of what we have observed so often in Wordsworth, i.e. the fact that the nature impression survives in the mind. This means that the way is open for retrospection and thereby the reflective recognition of the loss, of the crucial distinction between what once was and what still is – which, by the way, is the innermost theme of the completed poem.

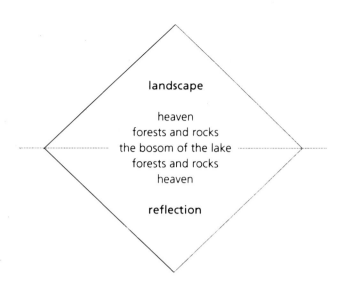

landscape

heaven
forests and rocks
the bosom of the lake
forests and rocks
heaven

reflection

J.M.W. Turner, *Lake Llanberis with Dolbadern Castle*, c. 1799. Turner Bequest LXX-X. As this watercolour shows, Turner at the very same time made similar use of reflection in creating a cosmic prospect.

The diagram thus illustrates the verticalisation of the fundamental structure of the boat image. As in the old poem a fall takes place from an original state, but now as a sinking movement. It is followed up – as in the boat poem – by an inverse movement, but the inversion now takes place because the reflecting surface of the lake is mirroring, throwing back, the landscape above in a vertical, upward movement.

That Uncertain Heaven

With this the retrospective element in the poem has decisively changed character. Whereas in the boat poem retrospection means looking back towards the starting point, in *There was a boy* it is the result of an unbroken process of absorption. The reflected image is meanwhile not entirely identical with the landscape it reflects, the surface of the water is not purely passive and receptive, but also active and transformative. The reflected sky is expressly called "that uncertain heaven" and thereby corresponds to the "touches soft" of the 1794 fragment, which of course denote both the vibrating surface of the water and the extremely sensitive and receptive, but also creative artistic mind.

Wordsworth scholars have discussed how "that uncertain heaven" is to be understood. Some tend towards the interpretation that the sky is transient, for ever changing in its aspect (the light, the clouds), while others maintain that the water is shimmering. In favour of the latter is Wordsworth's own use of the lake as a mirror in the 1794 fragment, where of course it is expressly the wind and the water that produce gentle lines on the image. But there are other similar, more or less contemporary examples which are not unambiguous. The reason might be that what Wordsworth is seeking to pin down is precisely not unambiguous, but the expression of a dialectic between nature and consciousness. On the other hand, the examples show how conscious Wordsworth is of the poetical potential of the mirrored image.

The most important example is found in *Home at Grassmere*, written March-April 1800, i.e. close in time to the second version of *There was a boy*. The simple image of birds over and on a reflecting lake forms part of the poem's profession of nature's diversity:

Witness the delight
With which erewhile I saw that multitude
Wheel through the sky, and see them now at rest,
Yet not at rest, upon the glassy lake.
(PW V p.331-332 ll.544-547)

The reflected image on the glassy lake is not an exact copy, for it is not still. In this it resembles the mirror image in the 1794 fragment and in *There was a boy*. And neither is it possible in these lines to decide whether it is the mirror (the water) or the object reflected that is the source of movement. The image is repeated further on in the poem, now with a clear indication of its being a portrait, not only of a landscape, but of universal nature inverted, reflected:

– How vast the compass of this theatre,
Yet nothing to be seen but lovely pomp
And silent majesty; (...)
Behold the universal imagery
Inverted, all its sun-bright features touched
As with varnish, and the gloss of dreams;
Dreamlike the blending also of the whole
Harmonious landscape; all along the shore
The boundary lost, the line invisible
That parts the image from reality;
And the clear hills, as high as they ascend
Heavenward, so piercing deep the lake below.
(PW V p.332 ll.560-562 and 571-579)

These lines from *Home at Grassmere* confirm the painterly significance of "touches" in the 1794 fragment. The reflected picture is "touched with varnish". Along with the word "gloss", the formulation unambiguously alludes to the art of the painter at the same time as the association with dreams clearly denotes that these "touches" are of a mental kind. Furthermore the passage confirms the interpretation of the landscape image in *There was a boy* as dual, consisting of a landscape and its inversion in a mirror image. It thereby also throws light on the actual mirror. For as stated directly in *Home at Grassmere*, it does not correspond to something static, but to something dynamic – a sinking down, a transformation.

The passage from *Home at Grassmere* is then yet another vision of the Sublime. The landscape extends between extreme limits, the hills, whose soaring movement is reversed in the mirror of the lake so that a powerful tension is created between universal forces moving upwards and down-wards. But the poem's display of these mighty, opposing expansive forces also illustrates that they are not separated from each other. On the contrary, on the basis of the reflecting and boundary-crossing central axis they must be regarded as dialectically related: "And the clear hills, *as* high as they ascend/Heavenward, *so* piercing deep the lake below" (my italics).[62]

In the movement downwards and inwards, the accepted boundary be-tween reality and dream is dissolved. In the reflection, the horizon – i.e. the difference between the mirror and the mirrored, the mind and the world – is dissolved. A fusion takes place of outer and inner in the same way as in several of the portrayals of meditative contemplation we have seen above, for instance when the mind is compared to a reflecting, but penetrable surface of the water in the fragment of *The Prelude* quoted earlier: "the calm/And dead still water lay upon my mind".

Read in this way, the extreme points of the landscape constitute a measure for the extent of the cosmic, sublime unity which is the inner-most significance of nature. A similar picture of a landscape is found in a fragment written some time between 1800 and 1806.

> A mighty vale,
> Fresh as the freshest field, scoop'd out, and green
> As the greenest billow of the sea:
> The multitude of little rocky hills,
> Rocky or green, that do like islands rise
> From the flat meadow lonely there -
> Embowering mountains, and the dome of Heaven
> And waters in the midst, a second Heaven.
> (PW V p.347: fragment iv)

Step by step the landscape cosmos is built up in a three-part structure corresponding to the one found in *There was a boy* and *Home at Grassmere*. Below: the valley with the hills and the towering mountains; above: the sky; and in the middle: the water that acts as the cosmic force uniting it all. This spatial structure might be considered a counterpart to Words-worth's earlier summary of the Sublime in the final line of *Simplon*: "Of first, and last, and midst, and without end". The water (metaphorically speaking) streams through the lowest part of the universe – the valley is like a wave of green and the hills rise like islands – and it mirrors the sky. This last function corresponds closely to the reflecting role of the water in both *Home at Grassmere* and *There was a boy*.

In the fragment, however, Wordsworth also plays on the character of the reflected sky as an earthly heaven or paradise and thus on the fact that the reflected earthly cosmos replaces the original, and now lost, paradise. In this way a third possible interpretation is introduced of the word "heaven" in *There was a boy*, to which I shall return below.

Common to the examples of reflected images seen so far is the fact that they visualise a sublime cosmic whole in the form of a symmetrical and dynamic dual image. Something similar is found in *Yarrow Unvisited*, 1803: "The swan on still St. Mary's Lake/Float double, swan and shadow". (PW III, p.84). As a total structure this symmetrical dual image is built up around a reflecting central axis so that the terrestrial landscape – the original paradise ("heaven") – doubles up in an inverse image. In *There was a boy*, this dual conceit links the landscape that existed immediately open to the boy's senses – his "appetite" – with the landscape that is imprinted in or sinks down into his mind. The progression from the upper to the lower, reflected landscape is the first step in a deepening perception and understanding of the world of phenomena.

With this, the poem summarises and explains the implication of Wordsworth's utterance that nature is imprinted in the mind. As the earlier readings have demonstrated, this means for Wordsworth that the original landscape is still present in the consciousness, but as a form inhabited by feeling. What *There was a boy* makes clear is first that this form is equal to, but not identical with, the original impression. Secondly that it is not static, but dynamic, as it imparts structure to the consciousness both when the consciousness is receptive (through sense impressions) and when it is creative or interpretative (e.g. through the meditative creation of images). And as a formative element it is not to be divorced from the consciousness it once formed.

In this quite simple, recurring image of a reflected landscape, then, Wordsworth sums up the understanding of the dialectical relationship between consciousness and nature at which he had arrived by the end of 1798. But as we have already hinted, the sinking movement in which the reflection is established, is not merely a fusion. The double image in *There was a boy* can be read both as a rhombus and as two triangles. What the boy unconsciously experiences as a sublime unity contains in the eyes of the mature narrator the seeds of a schism. The deepening perception and absorption of the image is also a fall. And so in this sense the reflected heaven – the paradise of childhood – is certainly "uncertain", impermanent.

This implicit and potentially disturbing aspect of the reflection in *There was a boy* is made explicit in the expanded version of the poem from 1800. It is undoubtedly the result of the work on the second part of *The Prelude* from May up to and including November 1799. For in *There was a boy*, just as in the longer poem, Wordsworth pursues his examination of the paradigm of loss and restitution and its poetical consequences. The new second verse in the 1800 version runs as follows:

> This Boy was taken from his mates, and died
> In childhood, ere he was full twelve years old.
> Pre-eminent in beauty is the vale
> Where he was born and bred: the church-yard hangs
> Upon a slope above the village school;
> and, through that churchyard when my way has led
> On summer-evenings, I believe, that there
> A long half-hour together I have stood
> Mute – looking at the grave in which he lies!
> (PW II p.206 ll-26-34)

Wordsworth has maintained the distinction between the adult and the child. They have now become two distinctly different persons: the adult narrator and poet on the one hand and the boy on the other. In this respect it is less important to decide whether the boy's death is to be taken literally or symbolically as the end of childhood; for the boy is used for the same purpose in each case: to describe the consequences of the cessation of an immediate life in nature – seen through the eyes of the adult narrator. The boy's death throws light back on to the first part of the poem, the most essential change in which is that the boy is consistently referred to in the third person. It could thus be said that the formal change in narrative technique from one to two persons corresponds to and fulfils the thematic development in which the boy begins to divorce himself from the original symbiotic relationship with nature and thus –

if we take the perception from *The Prelude* into consideration – with the mother.

This incipient divorce is – like the impression of the landscape – something that it placed outside the boy's own horizon of consciousness. Nevertheless the process is a theme in the poem because it is spoken by a narrator in an entirely classical sense, as is indicated by the first words: "There was a boy", once upon a time. Through hindsight and the distance he establishes in memory or observation, this narrator can see a significance in what the boy experiences in nature which is different from what the boy himself can see. It is thus now the narrator who sees the reflected sky as "uncertain". The childish consciousness has been superseded by an adult consciousness. Or rather: the boy's world of experience, which comes to an end with his death, is now known only through the adult narrator's re-creation of it in the poem. In this respect there is a question of a duality between childish and adult – not only in the final image in the first stanza, but in the poem as a whole. As such the added second part represents the development of Wordsworth's own consciousness of the complexities involved in the relation of the child and the man.

The interplay between past and present and between the adult and childish consciousness, which is already present in the first version of *There was a boy*, acquires greater significance in the light of the new second verse. It now determines the whole thrust of the poem, in which the balance between unreflected and reflected attitudes to nature gradually changes until in the second part of the poem the narrator explicitly emerges as such, meditating at the boy's grave. In this way the poem shows how the gradual advent of the adult consciousness is determined by the disappearance of childish attributes. The stages in this process constitute the basic composition of the 1800 version of the poem.

Put somewhat schematically, it is now possible to distinguish between three stages in the poem taken as a whole. *The first stage* is the boy's symbiotic unity with nature (the game with the owls), in which the boy is not conscious of any distinction between his own person and nature. *The second stage* constitutes the incipient schism between nature and the self, which meanwhile is only registered by the narrator (nature surprising the boy). As we have already seen, it is primarily in the actual structure of the final image in the first part that the hidden adult consciousness can be sensed. What the boy experiences as a sublime correspondence – because he has not yet consciously divorced himself from the surrounding world – is at the very same time the beginning of the division between the self and the surrounding world: paradise is no longer assured ("uncertain heaven"). The process leading to this division can be deduced from the order in which the narrator describes two stages in the boy's reception of nature: first the heart, then the mind. For this is no arbitrary order. The heart, i.e. feeling, represents an immediate stage and is also linked to sound, that is to say the child's earliest sense experience.[63] The mind represents incipient self-awareness and thus the boy's approaching divorce from the close relationship to nature, linked to sight, which is the sense associated with distance.

With this, the *third stage* is prepared. This is contained in the second part of the poem in which the complete separation of the (adult) consciousness from nature is marked by the silent, contemplating narrator at the boy's graveside and the picture of the landscape passed on by the narrator. On the slope above the school, where the young people congregate, the churchyard with the dead boy's grave is placed like a memento mori that silences the narrator. The boy's grave is emphasised as the central feature of the cultural landscape, because it is the interpretative core of the poem, the place from which all lines of sight secretly radiate and finally openly come together in the narrator's reflections. From this contemplation emerges the vision: the poem about the dead boy and the world that was his.

Although the poem evolves from the poet's meditation on the boy's grave, the poem itself is not created at the grave but literally beyond it. The scene with the poet at the grave is not only a recurring one, it is also seen or recalled from a distance in both space and time. "Pre-eminent in beauty *is* the vale", "I *believe* (...) I *have stood*". The poet is obviously not only recalling his former meditations at the grave but also placing these contemplative moments within a larger frame: the actual valley as it stands before him "now" at the very moment of writing.

So, whatever may be the relationship between the narrator and the boy and the time that has been lost – and on this very point the narrator is silent – the grave is a reminder that only in death do we again become one with nature. In the grave the dead boy has returned to the maternal earth from which he came. As the landscape sinks down, so, too, does the boy, down into the elementary, "steady" "bosom" that is ready to receive him.

But a limit is thereby set to any tendency to nostalgia or regression in the meditative narrator's relationship with childhood and the maternal, surrounding nature: what is lost is definitively lost in its original, sensual and physical manifestation. The grave is firmly closed around its contents, rejecting any meaningful intrusion or exchange. At this point the poem takes over. The boy's return to the earth, to nature, is the precondition for the inverse thrust of the poem.

For the narrator's silence does not derive exclusively from the paralysing conditions of the grave and death. It also forms the logically final stage in the great articulatory effort in the poem as a whole countering the irrevocable fall. The first stage of the process belongs to the voice of nature, this language before language which was the boy's spontaneous expression or which impressed itself in him – partly in the *unarticulated sounds of nature* produced by the boy and the owls, and partly in the sovereign *non-human voice of nature* that penetrated into his heart.

The second stage of this articulatory process appears when an individual personality emerges from this immediate relationship with nature and another language of a reflective, interior kind appears. The death of the unarticulated sounds of nature prepares the way for the growth of an articulatory potential associated with the mute narrator and his poem. In this sense a silent but visual form of expression – the written word – takes over.

So, the spontaneous, unreflective experience of nature encompasses its own irrevocable catastrophe in that it is submerged, while the imprint of it remains. For, as has earlier been suggested, this afterlife in the mind drags the retrospective and in that sense reflective, mirroring aspect along with it. This is given quite tangible expression by the poet closing with a last glimpse of the valley in which he places both the grave and himself.

Read from the first to the last line, the poem thus moves from a spontaneously sensed and imprinted landscape to a recalled landscape picture, from passive reception to creative imagination, from the boy's spontaneous "un-reflective" reflection of nature – via its imperceptible submersion and reflection in the lake or the reflective surface of the mind – to its re-emergence in the narrator's vision of the beautiful valley in which the boy was born and grew up ("the vale/Where he was born and bred"). With this retrospective panorama and with the use of the past tense "was", the picture of the valley reiterates the total range of the poem:

the boy's fate and the narrator's final position at the end of the story. As in *Tintern Abbey* the landscape is the same, but the observer has changed.

The implication suggested above can also be illustrated by the previous diagram of the symmetrical structure of the poem. If the upper triangle corresponds to the originally sensed landscape and the lower one to its impressed sublime form in the boy, then the overall rhomboid figure, where the borderline between the upper and the lower triangles is dissolved, corresponds to the sublime totality which is created in the grown boy's imaginative use – his inversion, reflection – of the original sublime mental impression. The pattern on which the poem is composed thus emerges in a repetition or reduplication of the form which the boy's mind unwittingly received from nature.

In this context, the boy's death – the end of the childhood world – emerges as a necessary prerequisite for the creation of the poem and thus also for the Sublime as an *aesthetic* form. This is why I have asserted above that the downward orientation from the upper to the lower triangle, the lake's embrace, represents a deepening understanding, the seeds of a mental transformation and in that sense also a fall from innocense, preparing the way for a new consciousness. This ambiguity can be illustrated if we view the sketch moving upwards from below. In an inverse movement – one that sublimates and crosses boundaries – the sinking movement is reversed, and what time has separated is gathered in a single dynamic image, a dual form in the rhomboid figure.

Reading the sketch and the poem in this way, we can talk of a twofold reduplication, two kinds of mirroring, a passive and an active. On the one hand there is the one taking place in the boy's mind, where the landscape is reflected on its surface (the lower triangle), on the other the recalling of this experience in the poem (the overall rhomboid sketch). In this special sense the downward movement of the boy (representing the loss of the world of the child) is the prerequisite for the emergence of the adult consciousness, whose sober acceptance of the conditions of reality and death make it into not only a consciousness of loss, but a consciousness of the necessary transformation determining consciousness itself. Thus the primal world of the child survives as the formative principle of sensuous and spiritual mature reality.

Viewed from this angle the final image of the poem – and thereby the romantic paradigm of loss and restitution – appears in a new and deeper perspective. The landscape which the poet sees before him as he writes is the same as the landscape in which the boy grew up. The poem's beautiful valley with the boy's grave at its centre thus contains another, older, and yet radiantly young landscape which is buried in the landscape of the present as its invisible archetype. And what applies to the poem applies to the poet too: the child is present in the adult as the unconditional foundation of his whole being. At once for ever lost and for ever present.

CHAPTER 4

The Light that Never Was. 1800-1805

The Child is father of the Man.

But yet I know, where'er I go,
That there hath past away a glory
From the earth.

William Wordsworth

Poetry's Perpetuum Mobile

There is a remarkable difference between Wordsworth's forewords to the first and second editions of *Lyrical Ballads* from 1798 and 1800 respectively. This difference is not the result of a more reflective relationship in 1800 to the volume of poems as such, because the principal idea that the elementary human quality is the subject *and* foundation of poetry became clear to Wordsworth only while working on the autobiography in 1798-1799. Although his words in the greatly expanded foreword concern the poems in *Lyrical Ballads*, the insight from which they spring stems from texts written largely after and partly at the same time as *Lyrical Ballads*. Seen as a theory of poetry, the foreword to the second edition is thus the fruit of reflection, the essence of which in all important respects is the meditative and imaginative forces revealed in the personal memoirs in *The Pedlar* and *The Prelude*, 1799. This dialectic between receptiveness and reflection – between what is experienced immediately and what is re-experienced in memory – is also a characteristic of *The Preface*, 1800:

> For all good poetry is the spontaneous overflow of powerful feelings: and though this be true, Poems to which any value can be attached were never produced on any variety of subjects but by a man who, being possessed of more than usual organic sensibility, had also thought long and deeply.
> (PW II pp.387-388)

The feelings which spontaneously overflow in poetry are preceded by a retrospective display of consciousness, something which can scarcely surprise anyone who knows the earlier work. Wordsworth provides a precise description of the process in the words immediately following:

> For our continued influxes of feeling are modified and directed by our thoughts, which are indeed the representatives of all our past feelings.
> (PW II p.388)

A kind of poetic perpetuum mobile is at work here. The feelings are edited and governed by thoughts which consist of former feelings, now filtered or transformed. Further on in the text Wordsworth describes this apparently circular movement when he expands the poetical principles contained in the foreword. Here we are confronted with the meditative approach associated with the experience of the Sublime in 1798-99:

> I have said that poetry is the spontaneous overflow of powerful feelings: it takes its origin from emotion recollected in tranquillity: the emotion is contemplated till, by a species of re-action, the tranquillity gradually disappears, and an emotion, kindred to that which was before the subject of contemplation, is gradually produced, and does itself actually exist in the mind. In this mood successful composition generally begins.
> (PW II pp.400-401)

In this way the process as a whole becomes a self-perpetuating dialectic.

The overflow of feelings, which is the precondition for the development of the writing process, is preceded by what was called meditative reflection in connection with the analysis of *The Prelude*, 1799, and related texts. But at the same time Wordsworth – entirely in keeping with what we have seen him do previously – emphasises that the feeling outpoured is not identical with the original one. A transformation has taken place.[64]

With this, however, it also becomes necessary to modify the model of the poetical perpetual motion machine, for it must mean that it has not set itself in motion. It has its primus motor; and this prime mover is the impression coming from outside and depositing some imprint, some feeling in a person's consciousness. This impression, then, stems from the world surrounding that person, from nature. What is moved, however, is itself part of nature. Put in a slightly different way: a person's elementary life is linked to the life of nature. This dialectic determines the rhythmically recurring three-stage sequence: impression of feeling, recall and expression of feeling.

In the introduction Wordsworth also establishes that the most important object of the poems is the real, essential, primary, elementary, beautiful and lasting elements in a person's "Humble and rustic life". In chronological order he talks of "the primary laws of our nature", "the essential passions of the heart", "our elementary feelings" and "a state of greater simplicity", reaching the conclusion about this simple rural life that it was chosen as a subject for poetry "because in that condition the passions of men are incorporated with the beautiful and permanent forms of nature". (PW II p.386-387)

It is this principle that Wordsworth formulates later in the foreword by using the metaphor of a mirror when describing the poet's own conception of the relationship between man and nature. In this Wordsworth – in full accordance with his own poetical practise in 1798-1799 – offers a striking secular re-interpretation of the kind of mirroring that is characteristic of the old Christian idea of the book of nature. Creation, nature as well as man, does not reflect the Creator but itself:

> He considers man and nature as essentially adapted to each other, and the mind of man as naturally the mirror of the fairest and most interesting properties of nature.
> (PW II p.396)

The mirroring quality in man depends on nature so to speak reflecting itself in man – and vice versa. man's elementary nature is irrevocably linked to nature's elementary forms and laws so that to man, man is himself a source of insight into nature, just as nature is man's source of insight into man. There are inherent, indestructible qualities in the human mind and corresponding ones in nature of which Wordsworth's poetical activities have given him an impression or impressed in him:

> I should be oppressed with no dishonourable melancholy, had I not a deep impression of certain inherent and indestructible qualities of the human mind, and likewise of certain powers in the great and permanent objects that act upon it, which are equally inherent and indestructible.
> (PW I p.389)

Such considerations are implied further on in the apophthegmatic definition of the essence of poetry: "Poetry is the image of man and nature". This is further expanded a few lines later in this way: "there is no object standing between the Poet and the image of things; between this, and the Biographer and Historian, there are a thousand". (PW II p.395)

The fact that there is no mediating link needed between the poet and the reality he is portraying in his poems is due to the close ties with elementary nature which the poet Wordsworth shares with his humble subjects in *Lyrical Ballads* – and which he had already examined in his childhood experiences in *The Prelude*, 1799. Wordsworth therefore also expressly rejects the notion of the poet as a kind of translator. Having realized that the distinction between subject and object, consciousness and nature, does not exist in what he writes or as he writes. Instead a rhythmical exchange or dialectic has replaced the boundary between them. In this exchange – referred to above as the poetical perpetuum mobile – man's true insight into his ties with nature comes into being.

We have been able to observe this poetical process in the previous chapter; now we meet it implemented in a written programme. Meanwhile meditative reflection no more operates of its own accord than it works without external stimulus. The poetical perpetuum mobile is productive.

So, in direct continuation of the assertion that the feelings are modified by thoughts which themselves are the result of such a process, Wordsworth shows, in his special variant of the doctrine of association, how the formation of consciousness is effected by the constant repetition of elementary experiences. The human mind – in this case that of the poet – is changed and expands in the process. But this also applies to other people's minds insofar as the poet passes on his insight to them. Poetry is endowed with the powers of enlightening and of purifying the emotions of its creator and its readers as well.

> For our continued influxes of feeling are modified and directed by our
> thoughts, which are indeed the representatives of all our past feelings; and, as
> by contemplating the relation of these general representatives to each other, we
> discover what is really important to men, so, by the repetition and continuance
> of this act, our feelings will be connected with important subjects, till at length,
> if we be originally possessed of much sensibility, such habits of mind will be
> produced, that by obeying blindly and mechanically the impulses of those
> habits, we shall describe objects, and utter sentiments, of such a nature, and in

such connection with each other, that the understanding of the Reader must necessarily be in some degree enlightened, and his affections strengthened and purified.
(PW II p.388)

The Poetics of the Sublime

In continuation of Wordsworth's explanation of how he came to choose the simple rural life as his subject, and thereby everyday language as the language of poetry, we find similar reflections on the significance of repeated experience. Here, too, there is an approach to elementary, supra-individual forms. But in this case it is a question of the actual language being capable of conveying these forms as distinct from the customary, arbitrary, poetical language – that is to say, a truly poetical language which does not translate, represent. In such a language nothing stands between "the Poet and the image of things". So, if we consider Wordsworth's poetical practice 1798-1799, the words suggest that he deliberately aimed at the essential language of ordinary people or children – dating back to the time of unrememberable being. Perhaps there are similar concerns behind fragments *(a)* and *(b)* in the *Peter Bell* MS 2 from February 1799. In the first of these, the poet talks of how, in the process of recalling, he seems to be speaking a universal language: "and, to my own mind/Recalling the whole picture, seemed to speak/An universal language" (N p.495 ll.6-8). The following, rather obscure fragment is perhaps an attempt to describe how in the resulting work of poetry the immediate, spoken language assumes an independent, objective form and substance; and furthermore how in its active function this language is related to the organic forces of nature.

> In that considerate and laborious work,
> That patience which, admitting no neglect,
> [?By] slow creation doth impart to speech
> Outline and substance, even till it has given
> A function kindred to organic power -
> The vital spirit of a perfect form.
> (N p.495)

To attain a true poetical language, then, is not a question of simply taking over or reproducing the essential language of ordinary people or children, but of hard work on the part of the creative mind of the poet. In the lines just quoted the poet seems to separate himself deliberately from natural forms in order to make artistic language work according to the same organic, simple laws as nature does. The poet substitutes the immediate forms of phenomenal nature with forms illuminated by the consciousness, the meanings imprinted by nature with the signs embedded in conscious, artistic language. This poetical process is what *There was a boy* is all about: the death of unreflected nature as the prerequisite of a language true to nature's inherent powers. In this way the vital spirit at work in the forms of poetical language is a function kindred to the organic power of physical nature. Thus the fragment and *There was a boy* both bear witness to Wordsworth striving to create an identity between the word and the phenomenon signified. Consequently Wordsworth sees mirroring as the fundamental form of the correspondence between them. The world of natural phenomena which sinks down in the bosom of the lake in *There was a boy* is resurrected in the reflected image of nature. This poetical process is the premise for Wordsworth's position in *The Preface*:

> Accordingly, such a language, arising out of repeated experience and regular feelings, is a more permanent, and a far more philosophical language, than that which is frequently substituted for it by Poets, who (...) indulge in arbitrary and capricious habits of expression.
> (PW II p.387)

It is such a non-arbitrary poetical language Wordsworth, in his own view, makes use of in *Lyrical Ballads*. Poetical language in this sense is not arbitrary or capricious, for it is always derived from the constant re-petition of impressed forms and feelings enabling it to catch and interpret what is common to man. Poetical language is the form of forms, the archetype of the emotionally typical.

So, when, in *The Preface*, Wordsworth speaks with such straightforward authority, this is primarily because his programme itself to a great extent rests on re-experiencing his own boyhood in 1798-1799.[65] He believed – rightly or wrongly – that the ambition to create a language that did not separate nature and consciousness had already been fulfilled as far as he was concerned. He had created a poetic oeuvre on the basis of the meditative examination of his own original, elementary experiences, and now he was fashioning a theory of poetry on the basis of this poetical experience.

The foundation for the actual theory of poetry is taken from the basic structure of this poetry: the loss of the original light and the attempt to re-establish it. For Wordsworth this simple structure corresponds to the archetypal tension between pain and delight which he identifies with the Sublime in accordance with contemporary aesthetics. The poetical perpetuum mobile in *The Preface*, 1800, embodies this very rhythm of original presence, absence and re-call, not least in the sense that, just as in the poems, there are two kinds of sublimity: on the one hand there is the original, elementary ecstasy in which the experience is imprinted and on the other the contemplative recall which derives its form from the original experience, but which at the same time infuses it with consciousness.

Seen in this way, many of the poems, for instance *A Night-Piece*, are not only about a recall of the Sublime, but of that kind of – derived, secondary – sublimity which is linked to retrospection and meditation and thereby also to the actual poetical process. In this perspective, "the spontaneous overflow of powerful feelings" is at one and the same time the moment of poetical inspiration, born of meditation, and the breakthrough of the secondary sublimity such as has been observed in Wordsworth's poetry: In that language grasps the Sublime, it becomes itself sublime. This dissolves the distance between nature and consciousness, past and present, and thereby in the idiom of the poem creates the desired presence – not as it originally was, i.e. physical, but as a presence in language, in the poem and thereby in the consciousness. All three derive their form and significance from what once was and – precisely thanks to this form – still is.

In *The Preface* the fundamental dialectic determining the poet's activity and world, is understood on the premises and key concepts of the Sublime as Burke and others long before had encoded them in the general cultured consciousness. "What does the Poet? He considers man and the objects surrounding him as acting and re-acting upon each other, so as to produce an infinite complexity of pain and pleasure" – which, however, completely in keeping with the tradition of the Sublime in the theory and practice of the 18th century, ends in "an overbalance of enjoyment". (PW II p.395-396) Similarly, towards the end of *The Preface* – and thus in a more craftsmanlike context – Wordsworth talks of "a complex feeling of delight, which is of the most important use in tempering the painful feeling always found intermingled with powerful descriptions of the deeper passions". (PW II p.401)

However, what Burke formulated in concepts, Wordsworth attempted to relate back to the elementary human world of experience in his great memory project. The Burkean concepts are thereby given a completely new and concrete significance in Wordsworth as signs of the fundamental rhythm by which all basic human experiences – and thus also the human consciousness – are formed and according to which they work. Wordsworth's ability to found his theory of poetry on the Sublime, is closely linked to the fact that for him it is the core of the law according to which human consciousness works. In this sense Wordsworth's poetry from 1798-1805 is a daring attempt to explore the sublime rhythms of his own mind as rhythms common to all men.

Internal Brightness

Nature impressions are not just transitory but indestructible in so far as they mould the consciousness. The impressions live on in the child's involuntary ways of interpreting its experiences and consequently – in the longer run – in the adult imagination. Here the original experience survives, not as content but as the form and language of imagination and memory.

This dynamic overall idea on which Wordsworth's poetry in 1798 and 1799 is founded, received its poetical and programmatic expression when Wordsworth finished the first version of *Home at Grassmere* in March and early April 1800. In this poem the valley with its natural scenery and its inhabitants becomes a kind of earthly paradise, not in the form of a bland idyll, but as a manifestation of the fullness of the individual life in good times and in bad, "the realities of life" (JW, p. 392, l.54) – which is also the fundamental theme in *Lyrical Ballads*.[66] This fullness finds its overall expression in another mirror image corresponding to those cited earlier in the interpretation of *The was a boy*, and which in this first version, in Jonathan Wordsworth's reconstruction, is a fundamental image of the totality constituted by the valley and the life in it:

> The birch-tree woods
> Are hung with thousand thousand diamond drops

Of melted hoar-frost, every tiny knot
In the bare twigs, each little budding-place
Cased with its several bead; what myriads there
Upon one tree, while all the distant grove
That rises to the summit of the steep
Is like a mountain built of silver light!
See yonder the same pageant, and again
Behold the universal imagery
At what a depth, deep in the lake below.
(JW p.409, ll.784-794)

Like the corresponding but far more elaborate image in the version in *Poetical Works*, this is also constructed around a vertical axis: the upward thrust in the tree and the distant forest rising like a mountain of silver light is balanced by the downward thrust in the reflected landscape. Like *There was a boy*, they constitute together a radiant, cosmic whole. This corresponds to an inner light in the poet:

> yet unto me I feel
That an internal brightness is vouchsafed
That must not die, that must not pass away.
Why does this inward lustre fondly seek
And gladly blend with outward fellowship?
Why shine they round me thus, whom I thus love?
Why do they teach me, whom I thus revere?
Strange question, yet it answers not itself.
(JW p.411 ll.885-892)

The answer is that he is a chosen one – "Possessions have I, wholly, solely mine,/Something within, which yet is shared by none". (JW p. 411 ll.898-899) This conviction that he is invested with visionary powers leads Wordsworth to make the daring proclamation that was later incorporated into *Preface to the Excursion*, 1814, but which in its original version sums up the optimism of *Home at Grassmere*. These forces are not individual in the sense of personal or private, but are manifestations in the individual person of the objective cosmic facts which arise in the meditative state:

On man, on Nature, and on human life,
Thinking in solitude, from time to time
I feel sweet passions traversing my soul

Like music (...).
(JW p.413 ll.959-962)

The listing of the subjects with which his poetry is concerned, culminates in a self-portrait: "the individual mind that keeps its own/Inviolate retirement, and consists/With being limitless, the one great life". (JW p.413 ll.969-971) It is characteristic of this portrait that the smallest and the greatest converge in it: the isolated, lone person of the poet and unlimited life. This gigantic range is yet another expression of the Sublime as the dynamic interplay of opposing forces, in this case the implosive, and the expansive ones. The poet's person is sublime – at the same time both minute and infinitely great.

As a poetical programme, *Prospectus* is obviously founded on Wordsworth's concept of the Sublime, not as an aesthetical category, but as a universal force. The vertical force pattern revealing itself in the dynamic image of the reflected tree, however, recurs as the basic metaphorical structure when Wordsworth marks out the direction to be taken by his ambitious poetical voyage of discovery, the object of which is to lay bare the powers in the human mind:

> For I must tread on shadowy ground, must sink
> Deep, and aloft ascending, breathe in worlds
> To which the heaven of heavens is but a veil.
> (JW p.413 ll.977-979)

Being unequivocal as a proclamation *Prospectus* at the same time seems curiously declamatory and postulational when comprared to Wordsworth's poetry from 1798 and 1799. It is as though the visionary power unfolding in these texts leaves him the moment he turns it into a philosophical subject and an explicit programme in *Preface* and *Home at Grassmere*.

The Child is Father of the Man

In two explosions of inspiration within a few days – from the 23rd to 27th March 1802 – Wordsworth wrote three poems: *To the Cuckoo* (23rd-26th), *My heart leaps up* (26th) and the first four verses of the great *Ode. Intimations of Immortality from Recollections of Early Childhood* (27th). The poems reveal the same fundamental experience, the loss of the world of childhood – the golden age, as it is called in the first of the poems to be written. Whereas in *Home at Grassmere* we find the lines: "in my day of childhood I was less/The Mind of nature, less, take all in all,/Whatever may be lost, that I am now", the poet's person is now separated from what was. The poems therefore seek to bridge the abyss with the help of memory. But they do not do this in quite the same way. Within the limited framework of time and text there is an interpretative change in the view of the relationship between nature and consciousness which Wordsworth had arrived at in his writings from 1798 and 1799. The change occurred when he in 1800 tried to endow the dialectics of nature and consciousness with monumental form in both poetry and theory – *Home at Grassmere* and the *Preface to Lyrical Ballads*. The ultimate conse-quence of this change, however, is only drawn in the final version of *Intimations* from 1804 and *The Prelude* from 1805.

The initial position in all three poems is retrospective and contains structural similarities with *Tintern Abbey* in the narrator being confronted by nature (in this case in the form of the cuckoo, the rainbow, the emergence of life in spring) and at the same time remembers himself in similar situations earlier. *To the Cuckoo*: "I have heard,/I hear thee", *My heart leaps up*: "So was it (...)/So is it" and – with a remarkable negation – in *Intimations*: "There was a time (...)/It is not now".

In *To the Cuckoo* the metaphorical foundation for the dialectic between the near and the far is not as hitherto the reflecting surface, but a new dual conceit, the bird's characteristic cuckooing which, as is well known, consists of a loud note succeeded by a more subdued tone rather like an echo. This dialectic unfolds in both time and space.

O blithe New-comer! I have heard,
I hear thee and rejoice.
O Cuckoo! shall I call the Bird,
Or but a wandering Voice?

While I am lying on the grass
Thy twofold shout I hear,
From hill to hill it seems to pass
At once far off, and near.

Though babbling only to the vale,

Of sunshine and flowers,
Thou bringest unto me a tale
Of visionary hours.

Thrice welcome, darling of the Spring!
Even yet thou art to me
No bird, but an invisible thing,
A voice, a mystery;

The same whom in my schoolboy days
I listened to; that Cry
Which made me look a thousand ways
In bush, and tree, and sky.

To seek thee did I often rove
Through woods and on the green,
And thou wert still a hope, a love;
Still longed for, never seen.

And I can listen to thee yet;
Can lie upon the plain
And listen, till I do beget
That golden time again.

O blessed Bird! the earth we pace
Again appears to be
An unsubstantial, faery place;
That is fit home for Thee!
(PW II pp.207-208)

In terms of time, the bird is a messenger from the past and the form of consciousness that was once the boy's: "Thou bringest unto me a tale/Of visionary hours" (stanza 3). As in *Tintern Abbey*, the natural surroundings to which the narrator relates are unchanged and consequently they remind him that he himself has changed. However, it is not the cuckoo as an individual bird that is the same, but its phenomenal significance to the listener. And this significance suspends the ever-flowing time which otherwise separates the two. In this sense and only in this, the bird is the same as the one he heard before (stanza 5).

However, the relationship is more complex than this. For if we consider the kind of significance and similarity the cuckoo creates with its cries, it, too, expresses a dialectic, though of a different, spatial kind. For the listener in the present as for the listening boy in the past, the cuckoo is at once distant and near ("At once far off, and near", stanza 2). What the cuckoo originally conveys is thus an ambiguity in life, based on the experience that what makes itself available to the hearing cannot be caught by the other senses. So what the cuckoo brings back to the listening adult across time is a form of consciousness, originally deposited in the child by the dialectic between what is and what cannot be conceived or retained by nature as a phenomenon.

This childish consciousness is strikingly reminiscent of what we have met in *The Prelude*'s picture of the very young, seeking, constantly border-crossing hunter, bird-nester or boat thief. It is a form of consciousness such as this that the adult narrator recognises in the course of the poem as a latent possibility in himself in encountering the cuckoo. After asking: "shall I call thee Bird,/Or but a wandering Voice?" (stanza 1), the narrator observes: "Even yet thou are to me/No bird, but an invisible thing,/A voice, a mystery;" (stanza 4). But there is no question of a sentimental fusion with the world of the child. What, on his own premises, the child had to try to discover by searching throughout physical nature, the adult, with his changed conditions, must seek by way of meditation, by quite literally lying down in nature patiently listening, until from within himself he can reexperience the golden age (stanza 7).

To an immediate view the child and the adult have, then, two different goals for their searches. The boy is trying to capture a being that can only be heard, whereas the adult is trying to reach the being he once was: the boy who innocently hunted what cannot be caught and retained. But seen in the light of the account in the preceding chapter of Wordsworth's view of the relationship between nature and consciousness, another interpretation opens up behind this, an interpretation that does not deny, but which from a higher perspective resolves the dissimilarity between the longing of the boy and that of the adult.

The adult's wanting – and being able – to establish a meditative link with the child's world arises because the longing for something that exists but cannot be found in a physical sense, derives from the child's experiences of nature. But to this must be added that not only longing, but also the adult's way of encountering the object of that longing stems from those same experiences as a child. As distinct from the child, the adult well knows that the cuckoo is in fact a bird and not some mysterious wandering voice. So when he nevertheless insists on the child's view, it is not a sign of deliberate naivety, but of his understanding that the child's behaviour is being repeated in him on a different level. For according to the narrator, the senses alone can not exhaust the experiences offered by nature. The child's experience of nature as something pointing out beyond immediacy thus contains a truth to which only the adult can consciously - i.e. reflectedly - relate. Hence the narrator's description of the bird's cries as "a tale/Of visionary hours".

So what *To the Cuckoo* portrays is the way in which the child's manner of experiencing survives in the adult as a sense of the profound mystery of nature, and thus the adult's route to experiencing nature as boundless - not on the child's literal, physical premises, but on the intellectual premises of the adult. And at the same time the poem shows how the adult recognises boundless nature by rediscovering his own original experience of the cuckoo within his own way of experiencing in the present. Thus the adult can continue to grow spiritually on that mysterious basis of growth which the child's world represents.

It is such a meditative, self-reflective process which is brought to completion in the last stanza of the poem, making the earth appear as it was then - in the adult narrator's mind.

Whereas the dialectic in *The Cuckoo* is illustrated by the cuckoo's twofold cry, Wordsworth makes use of a different image in *My heart leaps up*, using another traditional symbol of unity and the cosmos, the rainbow:

> My heart leaps up when I behold
> A rainbow in the sky:
> So was it when my life began;
> So is it now I am a man;
> So be it when I shall grow old,
>   Or let me die!
> The Child is father of the Man;
> And I could wish my days to be
> Bound each to each by natural piety.
> (PW I p.226)

As a traditional image the rainbow is first and foremost spatial in its associations, the rainbow's semicircle forming a bridge linking separated localities.[67] This spatial correspondence is also the fundamental element in Wordsworth's rainbow poem, but the significance of the spatial quality is temporal. The poem's adult narrator does not only react to the sight of the rainbow, but also to his own response. The sublime uplift, which lies in the heart leaping up, is not merely a suggestion of the semicircular form of the rainbow. It is also a repetition of earlier experiences of a similar kind: the physically present rainbow activates memory and thus reveals itself – like the cuckoo – as linked to a specific form of consciousness or experience. Thus in this poem, too, the sublimity rests on a deeply impressed pattern originally derived from the phenomena of nature but now living on as a spiritual structure independent of the original impression.

This mind-pattern, this form, is found both in the child and the adult. So as the poem proceeds, an intellectual rainbow is revealed in or behind the physical one. This rainbow manifests itself as a dialectic between then and now, the child and the adult – or, expressed in slightly complicated terms: the adult's reflection on the reflection of the child's mind in the adult.

With this spiritual rainbow Wordsworth seeks at the same time to retain the non-dissecting, uniting potential to reflect embedded in meditation, and to illustrate that this potential is again dependent on the fact that the ability to meditate and reflect regards itself as determined and governed by what it reflects (on). With this the rainbow becomes a symbol of inversion and thus a new variant of the reflection or mirroring that is the fundamental structure in *There was a boy* – and *The Prelude*, 1799, for that matter. But still another inversion takes place in the poem. The normal concept of the sequence of generations in which fathers produce offspring is turned on its head in the short and paradoxical apophthegmatic statement that the child is father of the man.

The Genealogical Inversion

In *Transzendentaler Idealismus Romantische Naturphilosophie Psychoanalyse*, 1987, Odo Marquard points out that the romantic idealism in a thinker like Schelling draws on the platonic idea that all philosophising is remembering, and that this act of remembrance deep down is an attempt to reach back to the time when we were one with nature: "alles Philosophieren besteht in einem Erinnern des Zustandes, in welchem wir eins waren mit der Natur".[68] In the case of Wordsworth, this sentence could without difficulty be extended to encompass poetry. Marquard further points out that Schelling radicalises this tendency by insisting that the task of transcendental philosophy is to make conscious this original unconscious condition. On this point, too, there is a clear agreement with Wordsworth's formulation: "the time of unrememberable being" and his efforts to explore the creative poetical ability. For it is done precisely by looking back in time to the close links with nature in early childhood and by bringing early experiences out in his writing from the dark into the light of consciousness.

In Schelling's case this led to a "transcendental method", which Marquard defines as genealogical. In my opinion the final three verses of *My heart leaps up* can be considered in principle as a piece of genealogy. Here, Wordsworth undertakes an inversion of the usual genealogical way of thinking in maintaining that the child is father of the man. This inversion can of course be read as a verbal provocation of the tendency still strong in his day to rank the child far beneath the adult, and it is possible that Wordsworth in fact had such an intention. But in that case it is only as a consequence of the more important fact that the wording introduces an intellectual or individuatory genealogy hidden in what is biologically determined: the notion that in his life every individual goes through stages of development that are qualitatively different and that a succeeding stage always presupposes and incorporates the earlier ones. In this sense the qualities of the child are contained in the adult as his precondition.

The line is thus a concentrated formulation of Wordsworth's own acknowledgement of the childish mind's fundamental significance for the adult consciousness such as we have followed it in the texts from 1798-1799 and on: the lost childish element has not disappeared but is still present in a form that is not of a sensuous, phenomenological kind, but constitutes an integrated, (normally) unnoticed part of the adult's potential for sensing, feeling and understanding. When the adult senses, feels and thinks, then, this lost past is already deposited in the actual sensing, and in the forms and dimensions of feeling and thought. This is exactly what Wordsworth expresses in a simple and serenely optimistic form in *To the Cuckoo* and in the introductory verse of *My heart leaps up*, where the heart actually does leap up. What the adult experiences here, he experiences thanks to a heart whose rhythm and mobility are founded on the child's earliest experiences of grand nature – in this case the radiant arc of the rainbow, where the entire spectrum of colours is gathered together.

Each in its own way, the images of the cuckoo and the rainbow retain the indissoluble link between the child-like and the adult, between physical nature and human consciousness. In one sensuous form they bind together what is otherwise divided into two, thereby acting in the same way as the reflection, the mirroring in the earlier work. They act as a form of memory, which, distinct from the current, nostalgic form, dissolves the boundary between past and present. One might therefore regard the cuckoo and the rainbow as a simplification and clarification of the mirror structure that has its most complex expression in *There was a boy*.

Thus *To the Cuckoo* and *My heart leaps up* represent a vital link in Wordsworth's formulation of the understanding latently present in the dialectic of mirroring or inverting. That is to say that the adult consciousness only lives because it is formed by the child's experience, while the childish form of consciousness survives only as an integral part of the adult's. As the melancholy narrators in *Tintern Abbey*, *There was a boy* and *The Prelude*, 1799, know, this relationship is no longer obvious to the adult. Phenomenon and significance are separated in the poet's reflective relationship to himself and nature.

Therefore the path to joining what has been separated goes not via a linguistic conjuration – analogy, metaphorical reconciliation – but via the phenomena themselves. For the relationship does not need to be brought about: it is there already as meaning in nature and that part of it which is the human mind. For Wordsworth writing around 1800, it is – as we have seen – not man creating meaning and then ascribing it to nature. Man's ability to interpret and comprehend the world depends on nature already having grafted significance into man. This significance is found as potential sublimity in nature, both external and internal. The mirroring and the dual figure come into this relationship both as physical phenomena and as a verbal form of expression for the same – sublime – reality.

As stated in Chapter 3, it is clear right from 1798 that this linguistic image is not an image in a mimetic sense, but is formed on the pattern which nature has imprinted in the receptive mind – and by the similarly formative recreation by the mind thus moulded. In the intervening period Wordsworth has become more and more convinced that this involuntary interpretative formation of and in the mind derives from a fundamental relationship between the creative potential of the mind and the creative spirit for which the phenomena of nature are an expression. In this way, the sensed phenomenon that is imprinted possesses a priori a significance which man can uncover step by step both in and outside himself – by way of his formed *and* forming consciousness. For the same reason this consciousness is just as infinite and inexhaustible as the nature that has put it there.

This conception of nature, however, implies a shift of emphasis from phenomenal to intellectual nature on the part of Wordsworth. This shift, which is to be discussed below, is almost imperceptible, for it takes place as a gradual transition within the same overriding concept: Nature.

From Phenomenal to Spiritual Nature

While this dialectic between nature and consciousness receives its simplest expression in *The Rainbow*, it seems to be undermined from one day to another in the *Ode: Intimations of Immortality from Recollections of Early Childhood*, the first four stanzas of which, as already stated, were written in immediate continuation of *My heart leaps up* or, to be quite precise, the following day, 27 March 1802. *Intimations* was probably intended as a continuation of the thought in *My heart leaps up*. This is supported by Wordsworth's subsequently using the final three lines of *My heart leaps up* as a motto for the final version of *Intimations*. The intention was actually realised, though not in the way one might immediately have expected. For Wordsworth appears no longer able to maintain his idea of the relationship between nature and consciousness. Thus it might be believed that *Intimations* – whether intentionally or not – reveals the self-contradictions which Wordsworth encountered when seeking to realise the wish expressed at the end of *My heart leaps up*. The wish for a life lived in respect for the natural invariability expressed in the realisation that the child is father of the man. This confirms the impression from *Preface* and *Home at Grassmere* that the nature dialectic was infinitely fragile for the very reason that it was not verbal but based on tangible experience. *Intimations* deals with the weakening of the visionary faculty.

The first four stanzas in the poem (which constitute the entire poem prior to the 1804 version) are like the preceding two poems built up around the loss of metaphysical dimensions – a heavenly light, a radiance has disappeared from the earth.

> There was a time when meadow, grove, and stream,
> The earth, and every common sight,
>   To me did seem
>   Apparelled in celestial light,
> The glory and the freshness of a dream.
> It is not now as it hath been of yore; –
> (PW IV p.279 stanza I)

However, in contrast to *To the Cuckoo* and *My heart leaps up* – and the texts we have read from 1798, 1799 and 1800 – the loss is irredeemable. In *Home at Grassmere/Prospectus* it is said quite unambiguously that paradise is here and now and that all searching for a transcendental one is vain.

> Dismissing therefore all Arcadian dreams
> All golden fancies of the golden age,
> The bright array of shadowy thoughts for times
> That were before all time, or are to be
> When time is not, the pageantry that stirs
> And will be stirring when our eyes are fixed
> On lovely objects and we wish to part
> With all remembrance of a jarring world -
> Give entrance to the sober truth; avow
> That nature to this favourite spot of ours
> Yields no exemption, but her awful rights
> Enforces to the utmost.
> (JW p.410 ll.829-840)

This confession of faith, for better or for worse, in the here and now is then given the following formulation at the end of the poem (in the *Prospectus* section):

Paradise and groves
Elysian, fortunate islands, fields like those of old
In the deep ocean – wherefore should they be
A history, or but a dream, when minds
Once wedded to this outward frame of things
In love, find these the growth of common day?
(JW p.414 ll.996-1001)

This new conception of paradise has fallen apart or is at least profoundly undermined in *Intimations* in 1802. The poem certainly tries to get around the gap between then and now by seeking healing in nature, as we have seen so often before. But although nature in spring tears him out of his melancholy in stanza II, the memory of what has been lost drags him in the opposite direction: "But yet I know, where'er I go,/That there hath past away a glory from the earth". (PW IV p.279, stanza II). And when nature in spring once more manages to outweigh the sorrow at the lost celestial light (stanza III and the first half of stanza IV), the pattern is repeated. In the texts from 1798-1800 nature is an effective antidote to loss and rupture, now it is taking the poet in the opposite direction. Stanza IV – and thus the first version of *Intimations* – ends where the poem begins, in irredeemable loss:

– But there's a Tree, of many, one,
A single Field which I have looked upon,
Both of them speak of something that is gone:
The Pansy at my feet
Doth the same tale repeat:
Whither is fled the visionary gleam?
Where is it now, the glory and the dream?
(PW IV p.280 stanza IV)

As the stanzas show, this loss concerns not only lost childhood, but in addition the loss of the meditative, visionary ability which the poems in 1798 and 1799 seem to possess – thanks to the fact that the childish experience there survives as the foundation for adult imagination. In contrast to that "tale" in which the cuckoo brings "visionary hours" back to the narrator, the corresponding "tale" of *Intimations* concerns the disappearance of the visionary faculty: "Whither is fled the visionary gleam?"

In *Resolution and Independence*, written between 3 May and 4 July 1802, Wordsworth approaches on this inner crisis from a slightly different angle. A poet who delights in nature one early, sunny morning, is snatched away from his euphoria by his hypochondriac reflections on what sorrows might await him:

> But, as it sometimes chanceth, from the might
> Of joy in minds can no further go,
> As high as we have mounted in delight
> In our dejection do we sink as low;
> To me that morning did it happen so;
> And fears and fancies thick upon me came;
> Dim sadness – and blind thoughts, I knew not, nor could name.
> (PW II p.236 stanza IV)

Sublime delight keels over into its opposite, the inner elevation is replaced by a fall which at the same time paralyses both thought and expression. Thus, the two poems, but mainly the second of them, both place the reason for the loss in the inner workings of the self. But there is also a difference, for the melancholy poet in *Resolution and Independence* is reprimanded and indirectly put right in his encounter with the old leech gatherer and his indomitable will to life. But reconciliation with the loss did not take place with such didactic ease when Wordsworth completed *Intimations* two years later, presumably in March 1804.

In the seven new stanzas to the poem Wordsworth returns to the genealogical viewpoint and expands it to encompass a whole sequence of stages. He describes the progress from child to adult as a series of repeated falls from an original state that was totally irradiated by celestial light, such as applied to the adult narrator in *Home at Grassmere*. Or rather: Man's soul is itself originally a gleaming celestial body. It is this light that is gradually separated from the soul and loses its strength until is pales so much as to merge with terrestrial daylight.

> Our birth is but a sleep and a forgetting:
> The Soul that rises with us, our life's Star,
>   Hath elsewhere its setting,
>   And cometh from afar:
>   Not in entire forgetfulness,
>   And not in utter nakedness,

But trailing clouds of glory do we come
  From god, who is our home:
Heaven lies about us in our infancy!
Shades of the prison-house begin to close
  Upon the growing Boy
    But he
Beholds the light, and whence it flows,
  He sees it in his joy;
The Youth, who daily farther from the east
  Must travel, still is nature's priest,
  And by the vision splendid
  Is on his way attended;
At length the Man perceives it die away,
And fade into the light of common day.
(PW IV p.281 stanza V)

I have quoted the entire verse so as to demonstrate the declining curve described by the graded stages of development. Read in chronological order they can be arranged as follows:

1. "elsewhere (...) setting" (the soul's condition before birth)
2. "birth" (the first decline: "a sleep and a forgetting")
3. "infancy"
4. "the growing Boy"
5. "the Youth"
6. "the Man"

As the progression shows, there is a significant change in the view of the child's development as compared to that found in *The Prelude*, 1799. Where the beginning was lost there in the early closeness to the mother and elementary nature (i.e. stages 2-3 of the list above), it here appears as the first element in what most of all resembles a neoplatonic myth of fall in which the divine light from the pre-existence of the soul with God sinks into the "prison-house" of material darkness, which thereby becomes identical with the light of the common day – in clear contrast to the earlier texts. The child's innermost being is no longer derived from its first months on earth and its intimacy with its mother and nature, but is established prior to earthly existence. Immortality is no longer synonymous with the supreme sense of infinity which is the child's before becoming aware of itself and consequently conscious of its own finite nature. Thus immortality must be understood as a qualitatively different form of existence preceding and following earthly life. Life on earth has become a parenthesis, where it was formerly everything.

The genealogical model, however, still applies; it is merely no longer psychological, but mythical. The child's psychological status as father of the man is inscribed in a neoplatonic myth of the fall – a spark survives in the child and the young boy ("trailing clouds of glory", "heaven lies about us in our infancy"). The rest of the poem is about these reminiscences and the potential contained in them (stanzas VI-XI). So the child has actually retained its role as the vehicle – or memory – of the original state. This original state, however, is not of this world, and in its birth and growing up the individual is taken away from it and led ever further into forgetfulness of the original glory – and in this case that means immortality – as it imitates the habits which adults have created on the premises of finiteness and forgetfulness.

Against this background the child appears as a visionary and prophet to the adult narrator, who finds himself in a darkness like that of the grave. But at the same time the child is blind to his own immortality, his own mighty potential – "blindly with thy blessedness at strife" (stanza VIII). At this zero point the possibility of reconciliation quite surprisingly opens up.

> O joy! That in our embers
> Is something that doth live,
> That nature yet remembers
> What was so fugitive!
> The thought of our past years in me doth breed
> Perpetual benediction;
> (PW IV p.283 v.IX)

Although the adult is subject to the inexorable law of forgetfulness, and despite the light from the star having faded and becoming one with the light of everyday, the poet is nevertheless able to understand that which the blind prophet is incapable of. For in contrast to what the poem has earlier asserted, there are in fact remains of the star's light in the adult.

This vacillation in the poem's light metaphor corresponds to the fact that the 1798-1802 conception of a temporal dialectic between nature and consciousness imperceptibly emerges again and encompasses itself in a neoplatonic frame of understanding. For in pure logic, the phrase "the thought of our past years" can only be understood as relating to temporal existence, since pre-existence is outside all time. Perhaps it is this inconsistency that persuades Wordsworth to introduce the passage by making supra-personal nature the subject for the process of remembering: "O joy (...)/That nature yet remembers". However this may be, the concept in the myth of the divine spark surviving in the darkness – here as the embers from the extinguished star – is fused with the idea that the past is present in human memory. Its source is, as we know by now, the impression created by grand nature, not during the pre-existential state, but in the very earliest days of earthly life: the early days of childhood. So the expressions later in the verse, "those first affections" and "the primal sympathy", which correspond to "those recollected hours" in *The Prelude*, 1799 (cf. the quotation below) can refer both to the surviving glow from the starlight of pre-existence and to the earliest childhood memories.

So in *Intimations* – thanks to "Those shadowy recollections" of these early impressions – there is a source of light in the adult which is "the fountain light of all our day,/ (...) a master light of all our seeing". This light has its origin in spiritual, cosmic nature and makes it possible for the poet to perceive "that immortal sea" which is his very origin. This process, in which cosmic nature becomes aware of itself in man, corresponds to the emergence of the sense which Wordsworth so far in his oeuvre has designated as the other eye, and which is closely associated to a light issuing from within. In the words quoted above from the end of the first part of *The Prelude*, 1799: "Those recollected hours that have the charm/Of visionary things, and lovely forms/And sweet sensations, that throw back our life/And make our infancy a visible scene/On which the sun is shining?". (N p.13 ll.460-465)

It is a related light we have encountered in Wordsworth's optimistic portrayal of the relationship between the adult consciousness and nature in *Home at Grassmere*, where the adult has a yet deeper relationship with nature than the child. When this light appears to return here at the end of *Intimations*, it is, however, only correct in a superficial sense. For until this moment in the oeuvre the inner light has been the expression of an absolute presence in the creative, visionary consciousness, an accord between inner and outer and in that sense total, boundary-crossing, eternal. But here, at the end of *Intimations*, the light has become eternal in the sense of immortal, extending beyond physical nature.

The poem's final reconciliation must be understood on these premises. When despite the loss of the original radiance the poet can nevertheless enjoy "the innocent brightness of a new-born Day" and in that find a "brightness" where in his literally dark moments he can only see a dimmed light, this all depends on the eyes through which the poet is now looking at the world. The poem is, of course, in complete agreement with the fundamental pattern of the sublime experience, formed as a rhythmical variation between depression and optimism, darkness and light, and leading to a sense of elation in which the light finally triumphs. So the person considering nature at the end of the poem is one who has realised that "that immortal sea" still provides the basis for his being. As in 1798-1799, the word sea is synonymous with nature. However, it no longer refers to the physical sea, "the murmuring sea that beats/Incessantly upon a craggy shore"[69], but to a metaphor, the immortal sea.

A rehabilitation of earthly life takes place on this basis. It is after all not boundless darkness, for there is still a sun for him who has eyes to see it. Logically enough, however, these eyes are no longer the self-radiant eyes of childhood – of the original sense impressions – but a cosmic immortal eye which at one and the same time keeps watch and emanates light from a sphere beyond the earthly:

> The Clouds that gather round the setting sun,[70]
> Do take a sober colouring from an eye
> That hath kept watch o'er man's mortality;
> (PW IV p.285 verse XI)

This eye is not the sensing, visionary human eye that colours what it sees, but an extra-human, divine eye – a sun behind the physical sun, which with its sober light testifies that there are caring powers not limited to man's finiteness. With this Wordsworth has introduced the very notion hitherto rejected of a paradise in a classical sense, a lost Arcadia beyond time and space.

The Revision of *The Prelude*

For this reason, *Intimations* forms a watershed in the oeuvre. Looking back, it is an expression of Wordsworth's not entirely consistent attempt to reinterpret the ideas forming the basis of his poetry from 1798-1799 until *The Cuckoo* and *The Rainbow*. Seen in the light of the later work, the poem is poised between the hitherto dialectic interpretation of the relationship between nature and consciousness and the lability which is characteristic of *The Prelude*, 1805. The genesis of this radically expanded work of memories is closely related to the change in understanding that takes place in *Intimations*. A reading of *The Prelude*, 1805 can therefore throw light on the reason for Wordsworth's changing direction here in the first months in 1804.

The completion of *Intimations* at the beginning of March 1804 coincides with Wordsworth's work on revising and expanding *The Prelude* to encompass five books in all, a work which in this final phase had lasted from January until the beginning of March 1804. Wordsworth's giving up his plan immediately afterwards and in the period up to May 1804 expanding his memoirs to encompass no fewer that 13 books (the original Book Fourth is divided into two) is, in my opinion, caused not least by the poetic self-reflection in which *Intimations* plays a decisive part.

Like so many others of Wordsworth's poems right back to the beginning of his oeuvre, *Intimations* is also about a loss of an original and glorious state and the attempt to overcome that loss. Wordsworth's answer to this classical Romantic problem is – as we have by now seen in a great number of texts – not a compensatory re-establishment in language, in poetry. Instead he insists that the goal must be sought, not in the object of the longing, but in the actual *form* of the longing, the kind of consciousness of which the longing is a result. This form impressed by nature is the form of the Sublime (cf. the previous chapter); and that is again the basis of the imagination which with its duality of receiving and creating combines nature and consciousness and dissolves the borderline between outer and inner, past and present in the sublime experience of unity. It is this foundation which to an extent hitherto unseen is questioned in *Intimations*.

In this sense then, *Intimations* is about a loss in loss, the loss of the very communicative ability which Wordsworth explores in his texts prior to

1802. It is thus a crisis poem. But at the same time it is also a kind of phenomenology of crisis leading to a liberation of the dimmed imagination – the other eye – in *The Prelude*, 1805, though expressly in such a way that this eye is no longer the poet's serene ability to see, but that of the infinite God or Spirit.

The poem's key position in the oeuvre is therefore not least dependent on the way in which it reveals the fundamental elements of the crisis in a clear form. This view is supported by the fact that in its composition, with its variation between depression and consolation, darkness and light, the poem incorporates the elements of crisis into the fundamental rhythm of the sublime experience: the repeated confrontation of opposites which finally gives rise to the Sublime reconciliation. Meanwhile, it is not immediately possible to discover the cause of the crisis merely by reading this poem in isolation. We must therefore turn to *The Prelude*, 1805, the genesis of which, as already indicated, is linked from the point of view of both chronology and understanding to *Intimations*, although the contents of *The Prelude* have come into being over a longer period. In this sense Wordsworth is speaking with two tongues in *The Prelude*, 1805.

The Moving Soul

Towards the end of *The Prelude*, 1805, Wordsworth sums up his work on the memoirs, whose driving force and most important subject is the imagination. In two senses, the development and transformation of the imagination thus constitutes the fundamental composition of the work – it is both subject and object. Nor must the concept of composition merely be understood in a technical sense, but as the very formative force or uniformity which has been dominant in the reminiscing poet's life and which appear when he portrays the life he has lived in both word and shape:

> This faculty hath been the moving soul
> Of our long labour: we have traced the stream
> From darkness, and the very place of birth
> In its blind cavern, whence is faintly heard
> The sound of waters; followed it to light
> And open day, accompanied its course
> Among the ways of nature, afterwards

Lost sight of it bewildered and engulphed,
Then given it greeting as it rose once more
With strength, reflecting in its solemn breast
The works of man, and face of human life;
And lastly, from its progress have we drawn
The feeling of life endless, the one thought
By which we live, infinity and God.
(N p.468 ll.171-184)

This retrospective and interpretative poet lists altogether five distinct stages from the start of the imagination in the dark cave and its further progression out into the daylight and nature. These first two stages are replaced by a third, crisis-like, in which the imagination disappears only to show itself again later, this time mirroring the human world. And this fourth stage finally prepares the way for the fifth, the poet's beholding God, the true, eternal source of all feeling and all thinking and eternal life.

In this way the composition – or, more correctly, what I see as the interpolated Platonic composition – reflects the pattern of fall and restoration and thereby the sublime rhythm of experience with its contrasting rise towards the vision or totality. But at the same time it describes a spiral, a return to the point of departure – the murky origins of the imagination – but now viewed and clarified from a superior level of consciousness. In this sense *The Prelude* reveals some striking similarities with the classical Bildungsroman[71], whose hidden principal character is the intellectually formative forces lying in embryo in the individual at birth, and whose gradual awakening is the true object of the developmental process.

The parallel is not a coincidence, for Wordsworth's autobiography or confession and the Bildungsroman are, each within its genre, consequences of what at the beginning of this book I called the metaphysical implosion. Since the individual is no longer inscribed in the basic pattern of history, it is vital that it should receive its own individual history and that this history should not be considered fortuitous, but be endowed with supra-individual significance. In this connection one might talk of the metaphysics of the individual. In Frank D. McConnell's words: "What has been heralded as the 'death of metaphysics' in the modern era is not, indeed, a death but the distinctly romantic growth of a metaphysics of the individual personality, a philosophy whose central methods are introspection and self-examination".[72]

Wordsworth's conception of the Sublime thus represents the secularisation of a traditional Christian concept of human identity. Firstly the conception of the Sublime, which he shares with his comtemporaries, moves the divine not only to physical nature, but to human consciousness and its innate potential. Secondly, to Wordsworth – and here lies his profound originality – the sublime pattern of experience is linked to the notion of man's development as consisting of a series of transformations beginning in the very earliest phases of life, from the period before memory, "the time of unrememberable being".

But Wordsworth does not leave it at that. The idea is inseparable from the unfolding of the imagination and memory, which for him are two sides of the same coin in *The Prelude*, both in 1799 and 1804-1805. According to these memoirs identity springs from an inner potential and evolves in a process which in principle never ends.

It is important here not to take a short cut to a post-modern or – as it perhaps ought to be called – post-romantic conception of identity. For Wordsworth and his contemporaries, human identity is not an arbitrary individual formation. It continues to be the expression of a superior, supra-individual order to which a divine status in a non-confessional sense is often ascribed. This supra-individual order is not represented by an earthly institution, a church, a codified sacred book, but it is manifested beyond any institution of human origin in the (inner) nature of the individual. Accordingly Wordsworth sees a correspondence between the individual and the objectively cosmic.

The vital function in this correspondence is managed by memory and imagination, the latter representing the visionary and linguistic actualisation of the first. The things remembered are profoundly personal – "each man is a memory to himself" (N p.100 l.3,189). But memory and imagination at the same time act through an originally impressed common nature which is not created by man, but is supra-personal, divine, the true origin of the personality.

Only insofar as man becomes aware of this potential – his "true" nature – can he fashion himself and his own life – or, to use two key concepts of his time, develop or form himself. And this recognition is brought about not by some external authority, but by the individual himself. The explanation of the central role played by memory is – as is obvious to modern readers – that individual identity depends on the products of memory.

As the vehicle for this epoch-making human discovery, Wordsworth's autobiography – and the bourgeois Bildungsroman, with which it has much in common – is a result of the metaphysical implosion. In their nature they are both expressions of a demythologisation and individualisation of the Christian myth of the Fall.

The similarities between *The Prelude* and the Bildungsroman can be followed through right down to the composition, which in both cases reflects the process of development in human identity. Like the typical Bildungsroman *The Prelude* is told by a narrator looking back on his own career viewing his life in three distinct phases. First the innocence of childhood, then the loss of innocence caused by separation of nature and mind in self-reflection and finally the attainment of a superior and conscious balance between mind and nature, individual and cosmic identity. The central and main part of *The Prelude* is thus focused on the protracted crisis that arises when the poet's self-awareness divorces him from original, spontaneous being. Similarly, the solution to this crisis is found in the mutual dialectic between nature and consciousness, the precondition for which is becoming aware of the individual's innate intellectual and spiritual formative power as part of (sublime) nature.

So it is no coincidence that in summing up his composition in the thirteenth and last Book Wordsworth the narrator alludes to the autobiography's metaphors for the development of the psyche: First the state of unity, birth and the very earliest life in the womb of nature (the cave, the water) before the light of self-awareness and awareness of the world enters and the individual steps out of the darkness of the cave. These two stages correspond roughly to *The Prelude*, 1799, and Books First, Second and Third as far as line 167 in the 1805-version, where Wordsworth explicitly draws a boundary. In the third stage, that of the crisis, the originally close relationship with nature is lost as the boy intellectually and physically moves away from the nature he originally knew experiencing difficulty in settling in the social world of the adults. As the reconciling power of the imagination is weakened, the senses and the intellect are separated and become equally valid, contradictory powers. The foundations of this third stage are laid at the end of Book Second and it covers the work up to the end of Book Twelfth, though in a rhythmical variation between passages where respectively the crisis-marked and the restorative dominate. The third and fourth phases thus appear in turn. This, of course, makes the actual order of stages in *The Prelude* less literal and chronological than the review of the composition in Book Thirteenth might lead one to believe. But it contains the truth in the sense that the crisis is ultimately overcome in a fifth and last stage in which feeling and thought are again united. The decisive event is the ascent of Mount Snowdon in Book Thirteenth. In immediate continuation of it Wordsworth lays down his overview of the composition, thus signifying that only from this moment is it possible to view – or postulate – the flow of the imagination as a total, purposive progression.

A Corresponding Mild Creative Breeze

The intention in the following is to expand this summary characterisation of the great and in many respects extremely diffuse work of memoirs and personal development by turning to a few concrete examples. These will then serve the specific, limited objective of illustrating the shift in Wordsworth's views on the connection between nature and consciousness as seen in relation to the preceding texts, not least *The Prelude*, 1799.

All the texts which we have read from 1798-1799 and as far as 1802 appear as variants of the idea that there is an elementary correlation between the person seeing and what is seen. This is found again in *The Prelude*, 1805 – apparently without change. In the Introduction to Book First, written in January 1804, Wordsworth thus establishes a very far-reaching dialectic between internal and external in the image of the breeze. This natural phenomenon replaces the River Derwent, which definitively loses its front position in 1804. The breeze comes as a messenger from the nature that greets the poet, now returned and looking back in memory, at the moment of his writing. This contact from without calls forth a response from within:

> For I, methought, while the sweet breath of heaven
> Was blowing on my body, felt within
> A corresponding mild creative breeze,
> A vital breeze which travelled gently on

O'er things which it had made, and is become
A tempest, a redundant energy,
Vexing its own creation.
(N p.30 ll.41-47)

With its retrospective first person narrator this section on "the correspon-
dent breeze" acts as the basic pattern for the entire interplay between then
and now in this poem, the attempt of the poet to retain the connection
with the world and the person he once was. His way leads via a thaw in
his frozen imagination, and its resurrection takes the form of a re-
establishment of the correspondence between physical nature and the
psychological processes in the poet, perceived in the cyclical rhythms of
nature.

With this re-establishment, the poet's restored link with his early
childhood in the remainder of Book First and Book Second is accorded
an inner justification. For with this the way is opened back to the child's
closeness to nature, which is the origin of the poet's imaginative powers
– seen now through the eyes of the adult. So if we read the lines as a
straightforward account direct from the poet's workshop, the formative
work on *The Prelude*, 1799 was generated by the force resulting from this
encounter with the nature he knew in his earliest days. As the imagination
harasses its own earlier creation, an inner storm develops, breaking the
grip of the frost and so making way for the burgeoning plants of spring
– "a storm/Which, breaking up a long-continued frost,/ Brings with it
vernal promises, the hope/Of active days". (N p.30 ll.47-51)

Taken in its entirety, *The Prelude* underlines and insists on this correspondence. As such the work of memory is a nuanced account of how
the dialectic changes as the relationship between consciousness and nature
shifts with the poet's physical and psychological development.

In the chronological starting point, the association is spontaneous and
entails no problems. We are already acquainted with its different variants
from the pictures of childhood in *The Prelude*, 1799, which are repeated in
1805. But in *The Prelude*, 1805 Wordsworth also incorporates older,
unused material as in the following passage deriving from his work on *The
Ruined Cottage* in January and February 1798. In the 1805 context the lines
refer to the redemptive potential which the memory of childhood's

144

closeness to nature contains for someone being devoured by "that mighty city":

> By influence habitual to the mind
> The mountain's outline and its steady form
> Gives a pure grandeur, and its presence shapes
> The measure and the prospect of the soul
> To majesty.
> (N pp.264 and 266 ll.722-726)

This is a version of the psychology of the Sublime that is strikingly reminiscent of Burnet's and especially Addison's heavy-handed linking of natural phenomena and the mind, and which does not come up to the more complex conception of the Sublime as an inner psychological phenomenon which Wordsworth had developed since early in 1798.[73] In another passage in *The Prelude* 1805, also deriving from work on *The Ruined Cottage*, though in this case February-March 1798,[74] Wordsworth describes the childish animism which the young boy grows away from:

> A track pursuing not untrod before,
> From deep analogies by thought supplied,
> Of consciousnesses not to be subdued,
> To every natural form, rock, fruit or flower,
> Even the loose stones that cover the highway,
> I gave a moral life – I saw them feel,
> Or linked them to some feeling.
> (N p.98 ll.121-127)

In 1805 the portrayal of this naive correspondence between nature's physical forms and the feelings is supplemented with the following lines which are in direct continuation of the preceding. Here, the process develops in the opposite direction. Whereas in the first part of the passage the poet received nature impressions linking themselves to feelings already existing within him, he now derives an inner meaning from the natural phenomena:

> The great mass
> Lay bedded in a quickening soul, and all
> That I beheld respired with inward meaning.
> Thus much for the one presence, and the life

Of the great whole; suffice here to add
That whatsoe'r of terror, or of love,
Or beauty, Nature's daily face put on
From transitory passion, unto this
I was as wakeful even as waters are
To the sky's motion, in a kindred sense
Of passion was obedient as a lute
That waits upon the touches of the wind.[75]
(N p.98 ll.127-138)

The concluding image has its roots right back in the earliest period of the oeuvre – the picture of the lake that both reflects and receives in the revised version of *An Evening Walk*, 1794. Due to the influence of nature the poet himself acts as one of the natural phenomena that have originally formed his individuality – the moving, receptive surface of water.

But a state of complete correspondence is no longer tenable. This already emerges unintentionally in the actual presentation when Wordsworth contradicts the image he has himself constructed by equating the lute – receptive, but explicitly man-made – with the water's surface. In this way he anticipates the inevitable outcome: that the balance between nature and mind sooner or later will be undermined from within by the progress of the poet's person in the direction of ever greater self-reflection. We have already observed this at the end of *The Prelude*, 1799 and in *Tintern Abbey*. In both texts a problematical distinction emerges between the poet's person and the surrounding world. This corresponds to the third, crisis-like stage in the summary contained in Book Thirteenth.

One of the clearest statements concerning this crisis is found in Book Fourth where Wordsworth returns to the picture of the mirror in a strikingly changed version. The reflection is formed as an explicit allegory of *The Prelude*'s own fundamental concern, the preoccupation with the past:

As one who hangs down-bending from the side
Of a slow-moving boat upon the breast
Of a still water, solacing himself
With such discoveries his eye can make
Beneath him in the bottom of the deeps,
Sees many beauteous sights – weeds, fishes, flowers,

146

Grots, pebbles, roots of trees – and fancies more,
Yet often is perplexed, and cannot part
The shadow from the substance, rocks and sky,
Mountains and clouds, from that which is indeed
The region, and the things which there abide
In their true dwelling; now is crossed by gleam
Of his own image, by a sunbeam now,
And motions that are sent he knows not whence,
Impediments that make his task more sweet;
Such pleasant office have we long pursued
Incumbent o'er the surface of past time –
With like success.
(N p.136 and 138 ll.247-264)

This pleasurable exploration of life beneath the penetrable surface is disturbed by the fact that at the same time the surface reflects the world above – the landscape, the sky, the sun and indeed even the very person doing the exploring. Thus the reflection has lost its reconciling, cosmos-creating function in which all differences between what is reflected and the person reflecting are dissolved. For the observing subject cannot exclude himself from what is being observed, which in this case is "past time". The world is falling apart. But this does not happen because the world has changed. The cause rests solely with the observing subject. Self-projection – which of course does not affect the boy or, at first, the young man either – only becomes an embarrassment when the young man seeks to find his way behind the mirror, beneath the surface, and thereby separates himself from himself and from the surrounding world.[76]

At this stage in *The Prelude*, then, the poet is separating himself from himself and thus also from his unreflective relationship to nature, and from the sublime form of experience as such.[77] But as the young man becomes conscious of his own hitherto spontaneous projections of the inner on to the outer and so retracts them, a very familiar problem arises: loss. Immediately after the passage quoted, Wordsworth also notes – with a formulation reminiscent of stanza IX of *Intimations*: "Those (...) Fallings from us, vanishings" – that something has been lost in the young man. He has fallen from a context and is consequently living a superficial, haphazard life: "There was an inner falling off (...)". (N p.138 4,270) The crisis has started, but as emerged from the overview of the composition, it is formed as a constant variation in which the poet's person is in turn in balance with and alien to himself or the world, nature.

Wordsworth places the first decisive breach with the balance of childhood and youth in Book Third.[78] This continues the portrayal in Book Second of the young man's early days in Cambridge. The passage including lines 1 to 167 was originally written in December 1801. When, more than two years later, Wordsworth proceeded to expand it, line 167 came to denote the end of the epoch in his life represented by childhood and early youth. As he puts it in the continuation, in words addressed to his friend Coleridge:

> And here, O friend, have I retraced my life
> Up to an eminence, and told a tale
> Of matters which not falsely I may call
> The glory of my youth. Of genius, power,
> Creation, and divinity itself,
> I have been speaking, for my theme has been
> What passed within me. Not of outward things
> Done visibly for other minds – words, signs,
> Symbols or actions – but of my own heart
> Have I been speaking, and my youthful mind.
> (N p.100 ll.168-177)

It is this inner world, which is immediately accessible to the child, but for the same reason difficult of access both to others and to the older man looking back – "in the main/It lies far hidden from the reach of words"; (3,184-185) – which now, with the necessity of age he must leave in order to proceed into another world, far away from the elementary closeness to nature and self-centred existence of childhood.

The Prelude, 1805, represents this as a descent to an inferior world: the intellectual life of Cambridge and then the city of London with its crowds of people. Both are universes created by human beings, and they consist of individuals isolated from each other, concerned only with the one-sided potential either of the senses or the intellect. This is described in immediate continuation of the portrayal in Book Fourth of how the disturbing reflection moves across life at the bottom of the water. The inner and the outer are separated in autonomous units. The passage thus deals not only with the establishment of the boundary between the observer and the observed, but also the change in view and its direction

148

resulting from this distinction: the poet and the poet's inner life become an object for the poet himself. And in this very twofold circumstance lie the seeds of the crisis which in *Intimations* and *The Prelude*, 1804 and 1805 are seen as a decline or actually a dissolution of the imagination and thereby also of reflection as the form in which nature and consciousness are dialectically linked. For it is thanks to the unhindered communication between the outer and the inner, between past and present, that the world has so far remained undivided.

At the outset the young man is confident, for as the image of the mirror in Book Fourth suggests, beneath this man-made surface is hidden the elementary fact that man is constantly subject to nature and its powers – despite his self-appointed material and intellectual authority. Furthermore these powers are deposited in man himself. In the individual memory, then, there is a source of insight into these forces. Provided that he is able to bring life to this inner source, his individual, personal qualities open up to a general, wordless and fundamentally incommunicable condition. Thus another, cosmic, breath is manifested in the poet's breathing. It is not he, but "it" that is drawing breath:[79]

> Points have we all within our souls
> Where all stand single; this I feel, and make
> Breathings for incommunicable powers.
> Yet each man is a memory to himself,
> And therefore, now that I must quit this theme,
> I am not heartless; for there's not a man
> That lives who had not had his god-like hours,
> And knows not what majestic sway we have
> As natural beings in the strength of Nature.
> (N p.100 ll.186-194)

These "god-like hours", in which nature breathes through us, correspond to the "spots of time" which emerge here and there in *The Prelude* as enclaves of light in the darkness of the crisis. This darkness dominates the rest of Book Third. As has already been said, the crisis affects the imagination as a communicative, totality-creating power. In short: "Imagination slept". (N p.104 l.260)

In a key passage in *The Prelude*, which was written immediately after the completion of *Intimations* in March and is part of the final "spots of time" passage, Wordsworth provides a clear formulation of the crisis of 1804:

> O mystery of man, from what a depth
> Proceed thy honours! I am lost, but see
> In simple childhood something of the base
> On which thy greatness stands – but this I feel,
> That from thyself it is that you must give,
> Else never can receive. The days gone by
> Come back upon me from the dawn almost
> Of life; the hiding-places of my power
> Seem open, I approach, and then they close;
> I see by glimpses now, when age comes on
> May scarcely see at all;[80] and I would give
> While yet we may, as far as words can give,
> A substance and a life to what I feel:
> I would enshrine the spirit of the past
> For future restoration.
> (N p.432 ll.328-342)

As in *Intimations* there is a motion to and fro between the restituting "spots of time" and the blocking of the access routes back or in. However, no sublime, reconciling movement emerges from this conflict, but on the contrary a desperate desire to retain what can be retained before the remembering poet finally loses the vision, i.e. his imagination, his visionary ability.

The passage has an unmistakable undertone of entombment and future resurrection, but in the form of a monumental stiffening ("enshrine", "restoration"). It is far removed from the happy passage in 1799 when, with sublime power, memory projects the life-giving sun of childhood back into the present. Poetically, things no longer grow forth of their own accord. As Wordsworth emphasises, man must himself contribute something if he is to receive the strength to achieve greatness from the fund which childhood represents.

But human resources are insufficient in this very respect. The visionary power which is the very foundation of imagination and memory inexorably disappears. This process *Intimations* describes as a gradual darkening of the original, true light. And what is more – here it becomes obvious that the desperation is not merely the result of the subject of the

150

poem being the person who is moving further and further away from his starting point as he becomes older. It also depends, to an even greater extent, on the fact that the person remembering is writing about this poetic self. *Intimations* provides clear evidence of this. For in this poem Wordsworth briefly looks up from his work on these demanding memoirs and formulates the conditions for memory thereby stating the reminiscing narrator's own position; a position which seems to be separated by an abyss from what is remembered.

Seen in this perspective it is memory itself that is under attack. As a restorative force it has become its own worst enemy. Each attempt at grasping what has vanished taxes those very powers which once ensured the living presence of what had been impressed in the images created in the poem. This vicious circle is born of a fundamental contradiction in the memoir project.

On the one hand the world of childhood is at once the object of memory and the foundation for the growth of memory and imagination, characterised by an original unity between sense, impressed nature and the child's non-reflecting mind.

On the other hand, the adult must necessarily rise above this immediate, spontaneous form of being. Consequently – as illustrated in the preceding – the poet's creative imagination is dependent on a loss, an absence. The ideal – and the solution to the dilemma in the expanded *Prelude* of 1805 – is to dissolve this absence in a spiritual illumination of the physical forms in which nature appears, thereby making it possible to return to childhood without receding into a second childhood. Wordsworth placed the "spots of time" passage from *The Prelude*, 1799, which of course is about the "renovating" ("fructifying" in the 1799 version) effects of memories of childhood, in the section forming the conclusion of *The Prelude* in 1804, which in 1805 represents Book Eleventh (lines 257-388). So originally the section was to act as a solution to the crisis of the imagination which is a major preoccupation in both 1804 and 1805. As in 1799, there is a question of recovering from the way in which the consciousness is worn down by ordinary, trivial life – "our minds are nourished and repaired". But in the description of the healing power Wordsworth adds a new feature in 1804, emphasising its uplifting effect. While renewal in 1799 consists of the elementary growth generated by these "spots of time", in 1804 the actual sensuous basis of experience is replaced:

> A virtue, by which pleasure is enhanced,
> That penetrates, enables us to mount
> When high, more high, and lifts us up when fallen.
> This efficacious spirit chiefly lurks
> Among those passages of life in which
> We have had deepest feeling that the mind
> Is lord and master, and that outward sense
> Is but the obedient servant of her will.
> (N p.430 ll.265-272)

The remarkable thing about this addition is that the sublime uplift at this stage is unambiguously determined by the senses' being subject to the control of consciousness. At the same time as these lines are being written, this necessity acquires an actual mythical form thanks to the neoplatonic turn taken by *Intimations*. That does not imply a fundamental change in attitude to the intellectual ability to abstract, which Wordsworth still considers false and secondary, but rather a further development of the meditative ability in the young man. Nor is there any question of nature having received a new, hitherto unknown spiritual dimension, for nature to Wordsworth has possessed this from the start. But a gradual shift of emphasis takes place from a dialectic between physical, impressed nature and consciousness to a predominantly hierarchical relationship in which physical nature is constantly subordinated and understood from the level of a superior spiritual nature. This shift is undoubtedly related to the fact that the subject of the expanded memoirs is this adult consciousness and the attempt via retrospection to maintain the link with what has been lost. But that is scarcely the entire explanation – as we shall see shortly.

The consequence is that Wordsworth, at least in lengthy passages[81] in both 1804 and 1805, reverts to a traditional hierarchical dualism between nature as a physical and sensuous phenomenon and nature as spiritual, divine, supra sensuous reality as is betokened by the neoplatonic elements in *Intimations*. In this context childhood with its "spots of time" does not represent a solution. Rather, it has itself become a problem on account of its confusion with physical nature and elementary sensing. So the outcome of the problem becomes the one we have seen in *Intimations* and in

Book Eleventh with its unambiguous subordination of sensuous nature to the spiritual. Thus a comprehensive spiritualisation of nature takes place in 1804 and 1805.

Breathings for Incommunable Powers

One of the clearest examples of this shift is the expansion which the key symbol in *The Prelude*, the breeze, undergoes between 1799 and 1804/1805. Its role as initial determinant has been described above. A homely nature comes to the poet in the breeze and reawakens his imagination and thereby acts as a link between the world within and the world without and between present and past. In 1799 this breath of nature has its origins in the tiny child's closeness to its caring mother. This trait is retained in 1804 and 1805. However, it now derives from a greater, divine, spiritual nature of which the mother's breath is merely the individual and sensuous manifestation. It is this underlying, non-sensuous, cosmic breath whose rhythm Wordsworth associates with the writing process, cf. the above quotation – "I make (...) Breathings for incommunicable powers".

Nature is thus in both a physical and spiritual sense "the breath of God" (N p.162 5,222). This emphasis on the spiritual aspect results in Book Fourth in the poet's soul being able to take over the active role of the physical breeze as an instrument for breaking the frost, when in his summer holidays he returns from his studies in Cambridge and the artificial, superficial life he has lived there:

> I (...) had glimmering views
> How life pervades the undecaying mind,
> How the immortal soul with godlike power
> Informs, creates, and thaws the deepest sleep
> That time can lay upon her.
> (N p.132 ll.152 and 154-158)

Continuing this passage Wordsworth describes how he is followed by a breath while wandering in nature – in much the same way as the young hunter in his childhood, the crucial difference being that it is now not the invisible, violated powers of nature that pursue the thief, but God who reveals His presence to the poet as he contemplates nature:

With darkness, and before a rippling breeze
The long lake lengthened out its hoary line,
And in the sheltered coppice where I sate,
Around me, from among the hazel leaves -
Now here, now there, stirred by the straggling wind -
Came intermittingly a breath-like sound,
A respiration short and quick, which oft
Yea, might I say, again and yet again,
Mistaking for the panting of my dog,
The off-and-on companion of my walk,
I turned my head to look if he were there.
(N p.134 ll.170-180)

This omnipresence, this correspondence with the most elevated, hidden powers of existence in the womb of the coppice is the intellectual reason for Wordsworth's spiritualisation of nature.

One of the consequences is that in a number of *The Prelude*'s newly-written descriptions of the correspondence between consciousness and nature, nature does not appear as a physical phenomenon – or to be absolutely correct: as (verbal) pictures of this nature, adopted into and interpreted by the consciousness – but as an express image, a paraphrase, an illustration. Nature is the "bodily image" of the supreme "soul divine", its earthly and sensuous manifestation for man. As Wordsworth, looking back, notes in the introduction to Book Fifth:

Hitherto
In progress through this verse my mind hath looked
Upon the speaking face of earth and heaven
As her prime teacher, intercourse with man
Established by the Sovereign Intellect,
Who through that bodily image hath diffused
A soul divine which we participate,
A deathless spirit.
(N p.152 ll.10-17)

Wordsworth has changed his focus from the unreflected, innocent consciousness associated with spontaneuos surrender to nature to the acute awareness of the transitoriness hidden in that same surrender. The narrator's consciousness of partaking in a divine, immortal universal spirit makes him at the same time bemoan the inability of his own spirit to find a worthy counterpart in the "shrines so frail" (N p.154 44-48) that are to hand.

Meanwhile, this longing for an adequate manifestation in physical nature of spiritual reality only finds an answer in the memoirs when on his journey to France and Switzerland Wordsworth crosses the Alps through the Simplon. His immediate response is one of disappointment. On the other hand, the experience – or the series of experiences – reveals that he has so far been looking in the wrong place.

The first stage in the process of understanding is his disappointment that Mont Blanc does not live up to the mental image he has formed of the famous and much-sung mountain. He experiences a similar disappointment when on travelling further he crosses the Alps without realising it. In both cases nature fails to live up to his expectation of the sublime coincidence of outer and inner grandeur which lifts up the soul. On the other hand, this rejection makes way for another possibility of an inner kind. Because Wordsworth is referred back to his spiritual powers and their innate, but slumbering greatness, which is now awakened:

> Imagination! – lifting up itself
> Before the eyes of my song
> Like an unfathered vapour, here that power,
> In all the might of its endowments, came
> Athwart me. I was lost as in a cloud,
> Acted without a struggle to break through,
> And now, recovering, to my soul I say
> 'I recognise thy glory'.[82]
> (N p.216 ll.525-532)

Whereas in *Preface*, 1800, it is symptomatic that nothing comes between the poet and the world, the poetical inspiration is now preceded by the fact that the sight of the earthly world is blocked. Only when nature has become invisible does true contemplation emerge. Imagination rises like a mist and blocks the poet's view of the physical landscape before him, forcing him to look inwards upon himself. In this form of inversion a hitherto invisible reality comes into view in the glimpses in which the light of reason goes out in both senses of the word:

> In such strength
> Of usurpation, in such visitings

Of awful promise, when the light of sense
Goes out in flashes that have shown us
The invisible world, doth greatness make abode.
(N s.216 ll.532-536)

Awe-inspiring forces manifest themselves in the incursion of inspiration or imagination. The sought-after greatness is thus not found in the external world, which is dissolved in the mist, but in the consciousness, which by dint of this dissolution can catch glimpses of a grandeur that transcends all reason. In short: the Sublime is the piecemeal correspondence of the spirit – human imagination – with invisible nature, the Spirit, God.

Wordsworth has thus not only moved away from his former localisation of the roots of the sublime in sensing, but also from his view that inspiration is an outburst of inner powers (cf. The "overflow of powerful feelings" in *Preface*). Inspiration comes from outside ("such visitings") and in bits. This reinterpretation of the potential force of the imagination, however, makes it possible for Wordsworth to find the answer he has lacked. On the road down from the unnoticed height, he finally encounters sublime nature. But it happens on changed premises: Physical nature is now only a sign for inner, spiritual nature defying description. We have previously read the Simplon Pass-section as a paradigm of the idea of the Sublime as it is unfolded in the nature poetry of the time. But what to a cursory glance looks like yet another mountain poem in the Sublime tradition, emerges in the light of the preceding pages with perspectives reaching far beyond pure, conventional landscape and aesthetical beauty.

Let us first consider the compositional principle of *Simplon*. It is a clear continuation of that in *A Night-Piece*. It rests on the confrontation of opposing forces in the sensing "we" – and this applies both to the detailed composition and the overall structure of the poem. The contrast between the constricting and the limitless, the rise and the fall, the chaotic and the cosmic, thus acts not only locally in the individual lines of the poem. For the individual contrasts act together in generating the poem's birth-like, basic rhythm of contraction, expansion, new contraction, new expansion etc. In four birth pangs of this kind the "we" of the poem leaves the narrow pass of the beginning and achieves the point where he can view the symbols of limitlessness.

The first expansive movement sets off from "this gloomy Pass" and culminates in the immeasurable height of the forests. But the expansive movement is complex. For it is also an internal vertical movement in that the eyes are raised up from what is close at hand opening up for impressions of the unlimited. The suspension of the fundamental contrast between the earthly and limited and the cosmic and unlimited in the expansive thrust is only momentary. For the contrast reoccurs in the description of the woods, which are at once in decay and yet indestructible. From this apparently unresolvable paradox the basic rhythm of the poem emerges: At first gravity wins over the expansive energy that seeks upwards in the equally paradoxical picture of the waterfalls, whose violent display of force stands there as the opposite: a static figure, an arc pointing downwards. In this image of the implacable strength that forces all upward movement back to its starting point, the eyes are also forced down, the field of vision is again constricted and the contraction ends in what is close and limited: "the narrow rent", dominated by the tumultuous confrontations of the winds.

From this point the second expansive movement sets in. The eyes are again lifted up from the limited sensations of the "twarthing winds" in the rent towards the torrents which – with yet another paradox – seem to leap from "the clear blue sky" in a vain rebellion against the static image which in the preceding lines made them into the figures of fall. "Vain" because the senses are again forced down towards what is near to hand, towards the sounds of the murmuring cliffs and the voices from the black, steep mountainsides running with the water that is incessantly flowing down from above.

Then the third expansion takes place. The sickening and dizzying sight of the cascading water, coming together and forming a rushing torrent, contrasts sharply with the sight of the clouds floating there, freed from their chains – an allusion to Prometheus – and the heavens. As in the preceding birth pangs, the expansion is directed upwards, though differently this time. Whereas the movement hitherto has been formed as an expansion of the range of the senses – primarily of vision – there is now an abstraction from phenomenal nature which has been prepared by the introduction of "the region of the heavens". A conceptual panning is enacted which sums up the contrasting and paradoxical elements in cosmic and metaphysical categories: "Tumult and peace, the darkness and the light". With this the poet gives universal significance to the concrete, individual experience of the overwhelming nature in the Simplon Pass. In this narrow abyss the senses, the eyes, are forced up towards the limitless and unbounded – and the same happens for man's consciousness which abstracts from the chaotic, limiting elements in physical nature and rises above them.

The contrary, contractive movement to this expansion is initiated at this point by the hitherto paradoxical and chaotic being joined together as features in one and the same mind and physiognomy – a physiognomy which thereupon expands in a series of identities in the fourth and final expansive movement. From being a "mind" and a "face", it grows into "blossoms upon one tree" which again is transformed into "Characters of the great Apocalypse" signifying the destruction of the earth. Freed in this way, the expansive growth can then continue into the eternal and unbounded ascending from what is sensuous, recognisable, individual and human to the incomprehensible – that which can only be intuited, not grasped. The poem's overall composition thus describes a progression from material and limited nature to spiritual and unlimited nature, from the individual and the earthbound to the cosmic.

Comparing this with the description of the early, intimate relationship between mother and child in Part Two of *The Prelude,* 1799, which was written at the same time, it is tempting to interpret *Simplon* as a reenactment of the experience of birth and the ensuing liberation from maternal ties. It is not accidental that the landscape in the mountain poem is also infused with elementary symbols of the female abdomen and only later supplied with male symbols. At the outset inspiration is literally "unfathered" (cf. N p.215 l.528).

To Wordsworth the Sublime as an *artistic* form of experience thus builds on the fundamental experience of birth and separation – and from the ensuing urge to interpret the loss which is prerequisite for the release of creative powers. Separation is then not only associated with irreparable loss, it is also a liberation and as such a necessary step in any (male) person's spiritual growth and thereby also in the birth of the poet, indeed of each individual poem. Consequently the Sublime in this artistic, conscious form is conditioned by the willed inversion of regressive emotional forces.

This very struggle with forces pulling downwards and backwards manifests itself in the poem in the flowing, falling waters of birth. It is however reflected in the overall structure of *Simplon:* the contrasts, the birth-pang-like rhythm, the repeated and victorious upward movement and the ensuing final release. This release is expressly not linked to the physical achievement: the climbing of the Alps, which of course is distinguished by its lack of sublimity, as noted by many scholars.

Read in this way, the poem is evidence of the huge, creative, visionary energy that is freed in the subordination of finite nature to the infinite, the spiritual. *Simplon* thus describes its own genesis – in a psychological and artistic, linguistic sense. The violent contrasts between which the poet's person is torn, and which express themselves in forces attracting downwards and upwards, backwards and forwards, must consequently be seen as the description of the process of inspiration. In this chaotic process the poet's urge for freedom and form breaks out and prevails in the sublime uplift from the darkness and the abyss, the narrow rent. Language grows out of unarticulated, tumultuous birth-giving nature as a formative, creative power. So the process, in which the poem is born, takes the form of a second birth into a world beyond the world of phenomena, another nature. As inspiration grows, a landscape develops from external nature: the latent, spiritual nature behind the physical landscape bursts forth.

To a cursory glance, the restoration of the imagination in *Simplon* might look like a return to the now old belief in a dialectic between mind and nature as we have seen it in for instance *The Prelude,* 1799 and *To the Cuckoo,* because imagination in *Simplon* seems to involve a significant correspondence between the inner and the outer. But to a closer examination this correspondence is a different one and in accordance with the new position Wordsworth takes in *Intimations.* For here in *Simplon* correspondence is not established between outer and inner nature, i.e. between the mind of the person experiencing and cosmic nature, but between an inner, individual nature and an unseen and invisible divine, spiritual nature making correspondence part of a hierarchical relationship in which the sensuous is subordinated to the spiritual. The passage of the *Simplon* thus is a daring attempt to visualise invisible nature "out of space and time" (cf. the quotation above from 5,45).

In this way physical nature loses its earlier role as itself and instead becomes an allegory of the meditative, imaginative qualities which are those of the adult poet. In one way this change is a return to the old notion of the book or mirror of nature in so far as nature's role is an allegorical one. But at the same time it differs markedly. When the allegory does speak directly about God in proclaiming sublime nature "The types and symbols of Eternity" – then this expression is itself allegorical, because the true subject is not God but the poet and his poem, as the preceding analysis has shown. In this sense nature has become the mirror image of the remembering poet and his spiritual potential.

This fundamental change can, for instance, be observed at the end of Book Sixth, where Wordsworth returns to two of his key symbols. One is the flowing water, which in *The Prelude*, 1799 has a number of related meanings: amniotic fluid, cosmic nature, the current of the river of life, the ability to remember, the river of the mind and the metamorphoses of the imagination.[83] The other symbol is the breeze, the wind, the storm.

> Finally, what'er
> I saw, or heard, or felt, was but a stream, a gale
> That helped me forwards.

Here, all traces of physical nature have disappeared; the words "stream" and "gale" are pure paraphrases for the spiritual, the coincidence of individual and universal, spiritual reality.

Acknowledging Dependency Sublime

The spiritual solution reached by Wordsworth in Book Sixth is not definitive though. In two respects. To begin with, the crisis returns time after time in the autobiographical but erratic chronology which in Book Seventh takes the young Wordsworth back to the city, to London. Secondly, Wordsworth seems to have certain difficulties in retaining his newly established position. The reason is that he incorporates old material without revising it, but this again is a symptom of his lack of resolution. This applies to the important passage already elaborated on from the end of Book Seventh, originally from January-February 1798, about the way in which grand external nature impresses itself on the mind and fashion it. In the new context the old dialectic between nature and consciousness acts as an antidote to the superficial, artificial, disharmonious ways of the city. But it appears in the midst of the new spiritual and hierarchical interpretation of nature. This contradiction is only resolved – on the premises of the work – when Wordsworth puts forward his solution to the crisis of imagination in Book Thirteenth.

The crisis only finds a solution at such a late stage because the contradiction between an originally total presence in the child's life with nature and the impersonal, unnatural ways of the city also encompasses the actual form of civilisation. So from Book Seventh onwards, Wordsworth tries to expand his investigation by viewing human nature as expressed in man's community-creating social activities, looking for its sublime potential not least in man's emotional and moral aspects. This attempt to expand the concept of nature receives clear, programmatic expression in the title to Book Eighth: "Retrospect: Love of Nature Leading to Love of Mankind". (N p.268)

The process is similar to that to which the relationship to physical nature is subjected in the early poems and the first books of *The Prelude*. It has the same characteristic three-part structure of loss and restoration as the corresponding earlier accounts, which for that reason acquire a more far-reaching significance. As before, the starting point is the boy's relationship to nature, which in his early years takes the place of life in the community and protects him from "the weight of meanness, selfish cares/Coarse manners, vulgar passions". (N p.290 ll.454-455) His becoming conscious of himself and his immediate relationship to true human nature leads to the dissolution of the immediate unity of feeling and natural phenomena, which for Wordsworth the narrator is identical with the first manifestation of the imagination: "that first poetic faculty/Of plain imagination and severe". But for the young man nature is no longer "a mute influence of the soul./An element of nature's self". (N p.292 ll.511-514) Instead a reflective distance arises in which the external and the artificial take control: "A willfulness of fancy and conceit". (N p.292 l.521) He is finally liberated from this condition in what, seen from the end of the process, stands as a process of ennoblement. It ends in a sublime unity which is a restoration on a higher, spiritual plane of what had been lost:

There came a time of greater dignity,
Which had been gradually prepared, and now
Rushed in as if on wings – the time in which
The pulse of being everywhere was felt,
When all the several frames of things, like stars
Through every magnitude distinguishable,
Were half confounded in each other's blaze,
One galaxy of life and joy.
(N p.300 ll.624-631)

The spiritualisation makes the cosmic into an allegory of man's share in an all-pervading higher existence which can only be grasped meditatively.

Then rose
Man, inwardly contemplated, and present
In my own being, to a loftier height -
As of all visible natures crown, and first
In capability of feeling what
Was to be felt, in being rapt away
By the divine effect of power and love –
As, more than any thing we know, instinct
With godhead, and by reason and by will
Acknowledging dependency sublime.
(N p.300 ll.631-640)

Instead of the evolutionary thinking that marks *The Prelude*, 1799, in which impressed nature forms the basis on which the boy can grow, another appears here which derives the inferior from an unseen superior nature. Man is not born of physical nature, but originally raised high above it as its crown, as is made plain by the neoplatonic myth in *Intimations*. Man's life is determined by a higher, spiritual power – "dependency sublime". As Wordsworth formulates it later in Book Eighth on the way in which the young man experiences the spiritual dimension in all creation, human nature is an expression in time and space of this higher nature, which itself is raised above time and the world:

The human nature unto which I felt
That I belonged, and which I loved and reverenced,
Was not a punctual presence, but a spirit
Living in time and space, and far diffused.
In this my joy, in this my dignity

Consisted: the external universe,
By striking upon what is found within,
Had given me this conception, with the help
Of books and what they picture and record."
(N p.306 ll.761-769)

In parallel with what has already been observed several times, the phenomena of eternal nature here serve an illustrative purpose in that by association they awaken a slumbering spiritual reality. The Sublime has moved further and further away from the concrete and can now actually be found in books.

From a corresponding lofty perspective of human nature Wordsworth in Books Ninth and Tenth considers his in many ways painful relationship with the French Revolution where he sees major and minor histories converging. The Revolution matches his dreams of freedom: "I pursued/A higher nature – wished that man should start/Out of the worm-like state in which he is,/And spread abroad the wings of Liberty, Lord of himself, in undisturbed delight". (N p.404 ll.834-838) Man must make himself master of his own life as a social being, but this striving, the basis of which is spiritual, is countered by the uncontrolled passions which the revolution awakens in France shaking the young man's notions of what is truly human. In Wordsworth's panoramic view the revolution assumes the forms of the Sublime, for cruelty, too, can be included in the pattern of the Sublime. By way of the violent confrontations between delight and pain which the revolution leaves behind in him, he emerges from the events with a greater understanding of the innate great forces in man – both those destructive and those of a superior moral character.

Imagination Restored

Book Eleventh returns to the starting point of Book First: living, breathing nature which is in harmony with itself. The breeze again appears in the reminiscing poet's invocation of the elemental forces of nature:

Ye motions of delight, that through the fields
Stir gently, breezes and soft airs that breathe
The breath of paradise, and find your way
To the recesses of the soul.
(N p.416 ll.10-12)

This is the start of yet another retrospective account of how spontaneous life is destroyed by the one-sided dominance of the intellect or the senses. Man is a dual creature: "the creature,/Sensuous and intellectual as he is,/A twofold frame of body and of mind". (N p.424 ll.167-169) In continuation of this, the programme of spiritualisation referred to above, with its unambiguous subordination of the senses, is put forward as an essential element in the repositioned "spots of time" passage: "This efficacious spirit lurks/Among those passages in life in which/We have the deepest feeling that the mind/Is lord and master, and that outward sense/Is but obedient servant of her will". (N p.430 ll.267-272) Childhood, so often lost and found again, returns once more, cf. the lines quoted earlier: "I am lost, but see/In simple childhood something of the base/On which thy greatness stands". (N p.432 ll.329-331) But this time the lines remain there as an imperative condition for the healing of the crisis-ridden, disintegrated imagination.

The question, meanwhile, is what the word childhood covers, as childhood here in Book Eleventh appears as the prerequisite of the restored imagination and thereby for the final establishment of the fourth stage in the composition. The answer is to be found in the stages of development already experienced. After a protracted crisis darkness is at last about to give way to daylight:

> Long time in search of knowledge desperate,
> I was benighted heart and mind, but now
> On all sides day began to reappear,
> And it was proved indeed that not in vain
> I had been taught to reverence a power
> That is the very quality and shape
> And image of right reason.
> (N p.438 ll.25-26)

We are here dealing with a spiritual nature of which external nature – once more – is only an image and not derived from it. To this nature corresponds the spiritual ability which Wordsworth names "the intellectual eye" (N p.440 l.57), and it is this that guides his work on the *Lyrical Ballads*. This ability enables him to turn to the world of ordinary people and see a superior, guiding, reasoning nature in their humble lives.

the forms
Of nature have a passion in themselves
That intermingles with those works of man
To which she summons him, although the works
Be mean, have nothing lofty of their own;
And that the genius of the poet hence
May boldly take his way among mankind
Wherever nature leads.
(N p.452 ll.289-296)

As in his autobiography he approaches the time when he began writing
The Prelude, Wordsworth also reveals the ambition that has driven the
work forward: The hope that this work, which starts in what is established
by nature, will turn out to be a power on a par with that of nature.

                              – forgive me, friend,
If I, the meanest of this band, had hope
That unto me had also been vouchsafed
An influx, that in some sort I possessed
A privilege, and that a work of mine,
Proceeding from the depth of untaught things.
Enduring and creative, might become
A power like one of Nature's.
(N p.452 ll.305-312)

Thanks to the spiritual abilities he has developed step by step throughout
his life, he has in his meeting with the everyday and trivial been able to
derive from them – and understand – a hitherto unseen "image" (N p.456
ll.360-365) of another world which could be conveyed to others.

I seemed about this period to have sight
Of a new world – a world, too, that was fit
To be transmitted and made visible to other eyes.
(N p.456 ll.370-373)

The basis of this imaginative power is the balance, the correspondence,
between inner and outer powers.

A balance, an ennobling interchange
Of action from within and from without:
The excellence, pure spirit, and best power,
Both of the object seen, and eye that sees.
(N p.456 ll.376-379)

This programmatic conclusion to Book Twelfth reaches back verbally to the dialectic that infuses *The Prelude*, 1799.[84] But the words about what is seen and the person seeing refer to a dialectic quite different from that in 1798. This becomes obvious in Book Thirteenth and the ascent of Mount Snowdon in the final Book, where the rediscovered harmony between the world within and the world without is sealed.

The Perfect Image of a Mighty Mind

The ascent of Snowdon is formed on the same fundamental pattern as the other descriptions of the sublime experience with which we have already dealt. Indeed, it shows great similarities with one of the very earliest examples, *A Night-Piece*, presumably because both poems are the result of the same concrete experience.[85] Both poems move from a state of (relative) darkness via glimpsed flashes of light to the coming of light. In *Snowdon* this movement is, however, formed as an actual ascent, which takes the poet through the mist and up to the cosmic vision. This encompasses not only the heavens, but also – in contrast to *A Night-Piece* – the panoramic view down over the sea of mist that enfolds earthly reality, and an opening in the mist through which this underlying reality communicates itself in the sound – the voice – issuing from the flowing, rushing water.

As always in Wordsworth, the picture of the landscape is based on a kind of geometrical ground plan with a central axis around which the landscape can be folded in symmetrical halves. And as in the later examples we have seen, this folding axis is horizontal, so that the world is divided into an upper and a lower part. Even when there is no reflected landscape, Wordsworth uses the fundamental structure of mirroring. Thus the landscape here is strikingly reminiscent of the image of the searching poet in his boat in turn seeing life on the bottom and the reflections of his own face as well as the landscape above him on the surface of the water. Beneath the sea of mists is the real flowing water. But in the ascent of Snowdon the crucial difference is that the separation between the person seeing and the thing seen is clear and unproblematical.

The gap in the mist represents the link with elemental nature. The fact that the waters sending their voices[86] up through the gap in the mist are homeless, results – with a significant shift – from the young mountain-climber Wordsworth having deserted them. The following meditation is the answer to their call. Just as this deserted world corresponds with him, so he corresponds with the waters through the link between physical nature and spiritual nature, which, as in Book Sixth, is born out of the mist in the process of inspiration.

While *A Night-Piece* provides material for reflection, but stops before it is fully developed, so the Snowdon text expands and interprets itself. This self-reflection is in perfect continuation of the tendency to produce an image of or to allegorise the description of nature which we have observed in *The Prelude*, 1805, not least in the *Simplon-passage:* Just as the sound of the water rises, a meditation arises in the experiencing poet, which makes the entire natural scene stand as something other and more: "the perfect image of a mighty mind". (N p.460 l.69) The definition of this mighty mind – as Longinus called it – is entirely in keeping with the 18th-century idea with its characteristic tendency to veil the borderline between the human and the divine. This mighty mind, which *Simplon* ends by describing, is in a field of intersection of gigantic forces which draw down from above and lift up from below. The mind is:

> one that feeds upon infinity,
> That is exalted by an under-presence,
> The sense of God, or whatsoe'r is dim
> Or vast in its own being – above all,
> One function of such mind had Nature there
> Exhibited by putting forth, and that
> With circumstance most awful and sublime.
> (N pp.460 and 462 ll.70-76)

So nature is not – as in the pictures of childhood in the early work up to *To the Cuckoo* – an elemental and permanent formative influence on the mind. Nature is an elevating illustration of divine, spiritual powers which already objectively exist. Grand nature does not make the mind great, but by the very analogy it makes the great mind awaken to consciousness of itself. Indeed, it even makes the lethargic mind sense and intuit spiritual greatness through the analogy.

> The power which these
> Acknowledge when such moved, which Nature thus
> Thrusts forth upon the senses, is the express
> Resemblance – in the fullness of its strength
> Made visible – a genuine counterpart
> And brother of the glorious faculty
> Which higher minds bear with them as their own.
> (N p.462 ll.84-90)

Nature's power to awaken is seen in the way it forms its phenomena. As such it is by means of yet another allegorical formulation related to the imagination, "the glorious faculty", which is likewise an illustrative and illuminating power. But the two powers are on distinctly different levels; their original balance has shifted. Whereas imagination for Wordsworth around 1798-99 and a few years on was primarily the work of nature, it is now unambiguously the mental power infusing nature. The imagery in the poem on the ascent of Snowdon is not least about this. The mind's correspondence with nature has become image-like, metaphorical, as also emerges from *Simplon,* which in the composition of *The Prelude,* 1805 is placed before *Snowdon,* but in fact was composed shortly after it.

In this chronological context the ascent of Snowdon represents a decisive new version of the mirror image. It is prepared through the dissolution of the earlier conceit in Book Sixth, where the mirror images appear as disturbing elements in the perception of reality on the bottom of the water. Now, in *Snowdon,* nature is the same as the great mind's image of itself, its reflection – the mirror in which the reborn, supreme vision, imagination, can look at itself. On this basis the final line of Book Twelfth on the dialectic between the seer and the seen must be understood.

Imagination, which restores and yet transforms, is still both receptive and creative:

> They from their native selves can send abroad
> Like transformation, for themselves create
> A like existence, and, whene'r it is
> Created for them, catch it by an instinct.
> (N p.462 ll.93-96)

But "they" – the mighty minds among which Wordsworth counts himself – are not bound by the impressions as was the boy in Wordsworth's earlier accounts. This applies for instance to the complex passage from *The Prelude*, 1799, which very significantly was removed in later versions. Wordsworth speaks in it especially of the tragic events of childhood which left permanent marks on his mind – "impressed my mind/With images to which the following years/Far other feelings were attached – with forms/That yet exist with independent life,/And, like their archetypes, know no decay". (N p.8 ll.283-287) Read together with the following quotation from 1805, this passage provides an excellent illustration of how since 1798-1799 Wordsworth has further developed his independent interpretation of the fundamental principles of the doctrine of association.

> By sensible impressions not enthralled,
> But quickened, rouzed, and made thereby more fit
> To hold communion with the invisible world.
> Such minds are truly from the Deity,
> For they are powers; and hence the highest bliss
> That can be known is theirs – the consciousness
> Of whom they are, habitually infused
> Through every image, and through every thought,
> And all impressions; hence religion, faith,
> And endless occupation for the soul,
> Whether discursive or intuitive.
> (N p.464 ll.103-111)

The community, the correspondence, suggested in these lines derives not from original nature impressions, but from the self-acting power of the spirit. To this power no fundamental contradiction between the reflective and the spontaneous, the discursive and the intuitive exists. From such a point of view the delight in natural phenomena and thereby the sublime experiences that arise in the meeting with grand nature do not derive from nature, but from the non-nature in nature. In other words: the communication between inner and outer is the spirit's internal communication with itself in various guises.

Nevertheless, Wordsworth does not only derive qualities like inner peace, freedom from fear, optimism, and a sure moral judgement from this spiritual dominance, but also an unfailing delight in nature as a physical phenomenon – "the external universe". (N p. 464 ll.114-119) Furthermore, he refers to the intensive closeness to nature in his early childhood as the basis for the human values which sustain his life and which ensure him against "a universe of death". (N p.466 ll.141) So Wordsworth's conclusion might on the face of it sound like a contradiction of all that has gone before. For the elementary, nature-given, seems here to be re-established in its former glory as the foundation of the Sublime. The following lines are thus an entirely classical Wordsworthian definition of the Sublime:

> To fear and love
> (To love as first and chief, for there fear ends)
> Be this ascribed, to early intercourse
> In presence of sublime and lovely forms
> With the adverse principles of pain and joy –
> Evil as one is rashly named by those
> Who know not what they say. From love, for here
> Do we begin and end, all grandeur comes,
> All truth and beauty – from pervading love –
> That gone, we are as dust.
> (N p.466 ll.143-153)

The core of this passage on the early life close to nature in childhood is unchanged from 1798-1799: it is love that is the source of all life and that which maintains it.[87] In *The Prelude*, 1799, the mother is the incarnation of this supreme innate power in nature. In a fragment from *The Prelude* from October 1798[88] this love actually appears as a life-giving, formative breeze to the child – as it also does later to the young man in the introduction to *The Prelude*, 1805. This maternal love is then presented here in Book Thirteenth in an archetypal or mystical form in direct continuation of the preceding quotation:

> Behold the fields
> In balmy springtime, full of rising flowers
> And happy creatures; see that pair, the lamb
> And the lamb's mother, and their tender ways
> Shall touch thee to the heart.
> (N p.466 ll.153-155)

But – and this is a crucial difference – here in 1805 this love is not the highest imaginable. And fundamentally, this is the same as Wordsworth implies in *Simplon*.

> but there is higher love
> Than this, a love that comes into the heart
> With awe and a diffusive sentiment.
> (N p.466 ll.161-163)

It is true to say of this higher spiritual love that it is a further development and a spiritualisation of nature's elementary (motherly) character. And furthermore, that it is coincident with the imagination whose intimate correspondence with what it observes and creates is the essential characteristic of love itself.

> This love more intellectual cannot be
> Without imagination, which in truth
> Is but another name for absolute strength
> And clearest insight, amplitude of mind,
> And reason in her most exalted mood.
> (N p.468 ll.166-170)

It is no coincidence that these lines introduce the retrospective compositional overview of Book Thirteenth and take the process of memory forward to its conclusion. At the end of the process, the remembering poet of *The Prelude* can look back on his life as it stands thoroughly interpreted by the composition of his own work of reminiscences. From this panoramic viewpoint the driving force in the entire process of remembering, i.e. the imagination, emerges and reveals its innermost being to him, which is spiritual love. It is nature's innermost, unreflective growth force which – where made conscious through human remembering – turns out also to be the guiding "reason" of nature, its spirit.

However, this spirit is not totally separated from sensuous nature. In *The Prelude*, 1805 Wordsworth drives imagination onwards to the point where it sees through phenomenal nature and thereby sees itself. In this process, the other, superior love becomes visible as the innate, hidden force in the former, and its meaning.

Wordsworth does not, then, deny that he has grown out of nature, maintaining the point of view contained in his earlier work and the first books of *The Prelude*, 1805. But at the same time he subjects it to a different interpretation when he maintains that the point from which the developmental process is to be understood is at the final outcome of the process, that is to say in the spiritual, the divine telos which precedes it in time and space. Wordsworth thereby expands the point of view from the neoplatonic creation myth in *Intimations*.

This is the justification for Wordsworth's being able to look back from the absolute spiritual climax in *The Prelude* over his work and the process of remembering and in this process to discover an inherent composition, the very dynamic which has inevitably brought him to this point. From this retrospective viewpoint the meandering stream of the imagination has been deprived of all arbitrariness. In his own winding, individual fate as a poet, Wordsworth on this last, fifth stage can sense the eternal, divine laws which determine eternal life, whereby he finds himself in harmony with the final verse of *Intimations:* "from its progress have we drawn/The feeling of life endless, the one thought/By which we live, infinity and God". (N p.468 ll.182-184)

Of Female Softness Shall this Life be Full

There is no denying that this is saying a great deal. However, this does not represent Wordsworth's final word. He ends in a far more humble position. The protracted, complicated sublime ascent, which forms the composition of the memoir and thereby his own life, does not result in contempt for ordinary life, although he maintains his fundamental spiritual view. The insight leads to a spiritual identification with the earthly creature from which he originally emerged, and which he has now so thoroughly scrutinised that his own identity now emerges in its right proportions. For Wordsworth this developmental process is completed in an imprinting of his own being – a spiritual bisexuality which from now on is inextricably linked to his poetical, imaginative activity. In this unity lies the innermost spiritual core of the Sublime. Wordsworth's subdued programme in Book Thirteenth sounds as follows:

And he whose soul hath risen
Up to the height of feeling intellect
shall want no humbler tenderness, his heart
Be tender as a nursing mother's heart;
Of female softness shall his life be full
Of little loves and delicate desires,
Mild interests and gentle sympathies.
(N p.470 ll.204-210)

At the end of *The Prelude*, 1805 the ability to love and receive love finds its way back to its source, not in an external sense,[89] but as a transformation of the reminiscing man's heart, his feeling spirit. And in this process, which is the final healing of the imagination, a figure emerges who has accompanied all the early work like a kind of guardian angel: the sister to whom the very first use of the mirror image way back in 1794 is linked, and who in *Tintern Abbey* represents his original self in a spiritualised form. In the sensitive, spiritual, sisterly love, at once both down-to-earth and elevated, are incarnated and united the two powers which the crisis-ridden Wordsworth in *The Prelude*, 1805 divides into the first and the second love – that which runs spontaneously from nature and that which later on reveals itself to the consciousness. As the third and final stage in this progression, which begins with nature's breeze breaking the frost and is followed by the melting strength of his own soul, the sister's spirit, her breath, has now opened the way – literally thawed the frost[90] – for the new growth which the poet as he looks back has finally experienced in himself as the innermost formative power in his life and thereby in *The Prelude*:

When Nature, destined to remain so long
Foremost in my affections, had fallen back
Into a second place, well leased to be
A handmaid to a nobler than herself –
(...) – thy breath,
Dear sister, was a kind of gentler spring
That went before my steps.
(N p.472 ll.236-246)

This sister provides the counterbalance to the loss over all losses in *The Prelude* – that of the first immediate closeness to nature with the mother.[91] Through the sister, his mental powers are redeemed and transformed: they are sensitively and tenderly directed out towards the world as it is, the here and now.

The sister's figure is certainly biographical, but it is possible to make a distinction between her and the significance which the reminiscing poet produces in his interpretation of her intervention in his life. In this sense *The Prelude* is not about Dorothy, Samuel and William or naked biographical facts, although much in it can be dated[92], but about meaning – about the fact that reality, including autobiographical reality, merely exists and only becomes real on acquiring meaning, i.e. as the interpretation of the powers revealing themselves in a person's life. Man cannot get around this interpretation. On the other hand man can have an interpretative relationship to himself as an interpreting *and* interpreted being by way of memory, as does Wordsworth in *The Prelude,* and so experience the archaeology of meanings, their growth in his own growth. The paths leading to and the consequences of such an interpretative, omni-revelatory human behaviour is the core of Wordsworth's work in the years leading to 1805.

Seen in this perspective, spiritualisation is not merely a denial of nature as a physical reality, or the result of contempt for it as such. Spiritualisation is much more an expression of the interpretative position which in Wordsworth's eyes is the irrefutable condition of man as a conscious being: that nature – including man's spiritual nature – always appears to him as interpreted nature, as meaning. Nature as such always suggests to man something beyond itself, irrespective of whether it is a question of a concrete, external or a mental landscape. This is a necessary consequence of fall or loss resulting from man's reflective nature. In this way the shift towards the spiritual point of view in *The Prelude* 1804 and 1805, becomes a logical consequence of Wordsworth's efforts to overcome the loss by pinning down the imaginative nature of the actual ability to interpret and discover significance – and its unbroken connection with the silent natural world from which it has sprung.

So neither must the clear emergence of spiritualisation in March 1804 in *Intimations* – an ode that is grandiose in every sense of the term – be seen as a sudden and radical breach, but as a gradual development of tendencies already present in the first texts from the 1780s. These tendencies even appear in the texts from 1798-1799, although there, of course, Wordsworth directly opposes the spiritualisation and metaphorisation of the relationship between consciousness and nature. For instance, the idea of the adult's daytime consciousness as a fall from a superior level of consciousness is present in the *Peter Bell* fragment from February 1799, where normal consciousness, littered with fragments of every conceivable kind, must be reckoned as "Relapses from that one interior life/That lives in all things". In this context it is important to emphasise that Wordsworth is not stringent and consistent in a conceptual, logical sense, and that his thoughts do not proceed in any one single direction. He is not and does not pretend to be a philosopher in the narrow, professional meaning of the word, but makes his way forward to new insights in his writings, hesitantly and tentatively.

The Prelude is thus the product of a passionate desire on the part of Wordsworth constantly to interpret and reinterpret what has already been interpreted, a thirst for meaning, which is doubtless deeply personally motivated. All the texts we have read provide evidence of this. But this passion derives also from the loss of meaning which the metaphysical implosion threatened. In this respect it is at the same time typical of the age. This, too, is borne out by the texts we have read. The metaphysical implosion undermines the view that God is the explanation and justification for everything, and in its furthest consequence it places man himself and his own interpretative powers in place of the divine order. The individual thus becomes the vehicle for the burden of explanation which the Church had formerly carried. From this context springs Wordsworth's basic conception of man as a significance-creating being who is able to interpret thanks to the fact that he himself is interpreted, formed. One of the elements resulting from this is the need to immortalise the very powers of the human spirit in the origin myth in *Intimations*.

Wordsworth's exploration of the Sublime as the supra-individual basic form of the consciousness represents a median position between a rejection of the individual, the subjective, and a radical individualism. The entire crisis section in *The Prelude* can thus (also) be read as an attempt to find the way to a balance between subjective and objective, concrete individual experience and cosmic affiliation, against a background of untenable infantile egocentricity and the equally untenable vacillation between crude materialism and abstract intellectualism. Both personal and supra-personal echoes of the time are thus to be found in Wordsworth, but in such a way that the path to general applicability – which for him is the same as the basic sublime, cosmic pattern – goes via the individual,

and not vice versa. The elevated can only be reached via concrete individual memory and personal visionary power.

So at the conclusion of Book Thirteenth and his memoirs, Wordsworth
can see his bold ambition fulfilled: the ambition of interpreting his own
nature until he reaches the point where his personal development is
proclaimed as the fulfilled individualisation of an originally inarticulate,
unconscious nature. And as the originally unrecognised emergence into
consciousness of the fashioning or interpretation of which this state is the
expression.

> Prophets of Nature, we to them will speak
> A lasting inspiration, sanctified
> By reason and truth; what we have loved
> Others will love, and we may teach them how:
> Instruct them how the mind of man becomes
> A thousand times more beautiful than the earth
> On which he dwells, above this frame of things
> (...)
> In beauty exalted, as it is itself
> Of substance and of fabric more divine.
> (N p.482 ll.442-452)

Wordsworth's dream of making his poetry into a kind of sublime interpretative power in line with that of nature is here fulfilled. This similarity
is dependent on an inequality – the poem ends with a description of a
consciousness more beautiful and more divine than the nature from
which it has been separated. Indeed, it receives its beauty precisely on
account of this separation. Meanwhile, this does not mean that the
speaker or writer has in an absolute sense divorced himself from what he
is talking about, but that the nature with which he was once silently
united is something with which he has now again become united as its
consciousness – through imagination. Beautiful or sublime nature is no
longer what is revealed to the senses, but spiritual nature or nature illuminated by the spirit.

The Light that Never Was
So Wordsworth's original poetical relationship with the Sublime in 1798
does not receive its epoch-making significance because his poetry provides

176

original formulations for the Sublime in a philosophical and conceptual sense, but precisely because he derives his understanding poetically from what is concrete and individual, what has been lived and experienced. It is this position which begins seriously to disintegrate in the spring of 1804, as can be detected in *Intimations*, his work on *The Prelude* and in the following passage from *The Excursion*, IX ll.440-442, written in 1804:

> In a deep pool, by happy chance we saw
> A twofold image; on a grassy bank
> A snow-white ram, and in the crystal flood
> Another and the same! Most beautiful (...)
> The breathing creature stood; as beautiful,
> Beneath him, showed his shadowy counterpart.
> Each had his glowing mountains, each his sky,
> And each seemed centre of his own fair world:
> Antipodes unconscious of each other,
> Yet, in partition, with their several spheres,
> Blended in perfect stillness, to our sight!
> (PW V p.300 ll.439-451)

The image of the mirrored ram is reflected, double in more than one sense. On the one hand there is the dumb animal which is the autistic centre of its own cosmos and in this sense an entire world. Indeed, the entire world is his. On the other there are the observers, the narrative "we"'s sympathetic understanding of the ram's being unaware of its own reflection. They are not only aware of the ram's non-reflective, innocent form of un-consciousness ("each seemed centre of his own fair world"), but also of the infinitely wide world which that innocense excludes ("Antipodes unconscious of each other"). However, in pointing to what is excluded, the observers at the same time point to the reflecting, dual form which consciousness of the infinitely great world inevitably brings with it. What the ram has no sense of, is appreciated by the observers: the reflection *as* reflection, as a doubling of the phenomena of the world ("Yet in partition, with their several spheres,/Blended in perfect stilness to our sight"). Thus the observers are not only conscious of the animal and its world, in observing they are also conscious of themselves *as* observers, as being apart from what they sense and interpret, as the concluding words "to our sight" confirm.

This particular mirror-image differs markedly from those from 1798 until about 1802 in being not so much a vision of cosmic unity or correspondence as a reminder of the inevitable dualisation of the world involved in the loss of innocense and the genesis of self-awareness, self-reflection. The mirror-reflection, thus understood, surely represents an expanded consciousness, but at the same time also a dualisation of the world – which of course is only divided for the person who can stand back from himself in contemplation. In this respect the mirrored ram is the mirror-image of the observers themselves. It reflects their way of sensing the world. They see in the ram what they are not any more, but once were: one with nature, unreflecting. In this way Wordsworth by simple means shows that in sensing the grown-up, self-reflecting individual interprets: we are always involved in, part of what we see – we cannot discern what is seen from the one who sees.

In another manuscript from c.1805 the passage is supplied with a very significant ending in which the observer has become an "I":

> A stray temptation seized me to dissolve
> The vision, but I could not, and the stone
> Snatched up for that intent dropped from my hand.
> (N p.506 ll.25-27)

It is not possible to decide whether the destructive drive aims at the vision as an image of innocent unity or an image of the duplicity inherent in self-awareness. Correspondingly it is uncertain whether the narrator goes back on his spontaneous urge because he cannot bear to erase the fond deceit or because he realises that the image, being a mirror image of his own way of perceiving the world, cannot be shattered by throwing a stone. The important point, however, is that in either case, the temptation arises in a mind far beyond the state of primal innocense – a mind unable to part with the recurring experience of duplicity as the basic condition of self-awareness.

The conflict suggested by the lines about the snow-white ram is openly displayed and named in a strikingly programmatic form in *Elegiac Stanzas Suggested by a Picture of Peele Castle in a Storm Painted by Sir George Beaumont*, 1805. The poem was written shortly after the death at sea of Wordsworth's brother John, about which Wordsworth was informed five days later, on 11 February 1805. Meanwhile, Wordsworth does not only take indirect leave of his brother in the poem, but he also takes explicit leave of the imagery bearing the nature dialectic arrived at in 1798-1799.

Beaumont's picture is a classical portrayal of the Sublime such as can also be found in the young Turner. It is this traditional view that Wordsworth has sought to transcend in large parts of his work so far. And indeed, the poem does open with an alternative view of the ancient castle – "thou rugged Pile" – as an expression of the sublime.

> I was thy neighbour once, thou rugged Pile!
> Four summer weeks I dwelt in sight of thee:
> I saw thee every day, and all the while
> Thy Form was sleeping on a glassy sea.
>
> So pure the sky, so quiet was the air!
> So like, so very like, was day to day!
> Whene'er I looked, thy Image still was there;
> It trembled, but it never passed away.
> (PW IV pp.258-259 stanzas 1 and 2)

The sun-drenched picture of the reflected castle in the trembling, receptive water is not only an alternative to Beaumont's but as such at the same time the simplest conceivable summing up of Wordsworth's visionary presentation of the Sublime. It is thus the fundamental symmetrical pattern of the early work that we meet in the first two stanzas. But it is depicted with an almost imperceptible platonic twist. Beneath the tangible castle sleeps its spiritually serene, permanent Form. All the greater is the shock when during the course of the poem the reader discovers that this imperishable form ("it never passed away") is a dream, an illusion.

In the following verses Wordsworth describes how, had he been Beaumont, he would have treated the motif:

> Ah! THEN, if mine had been the Painter's hand,
> To express what then I saw; and add the gleam,
> The light that never was, on sea or land,
> The consecration, and the Poet's dream;
>
> I would have planted thee, thou hoary Pile
> Amid a world how different from this!
> Beside a sea that could not cease to smile;
> On tranquil land, beneath a sky of bliss.

Thou shouldst have seemed a treasure-house divine
Of peaceful years; a chronicle of heaven; –
Of all the sunbeams that did every shine
The very sweetest had to be thee given.

A picture had it been of lasting ease
Elysian quiet, without toil or strife;
No motion but the moving tide, a breeze,
Or merely silent Nature's breathing life.
(stanzas 4-7)

The lines are a veritable compendium of the nature elements and the fundamental meditative mood that help make up Wordsworth's poetry on the Sublime: light, sunbeams, sea, land, sky, heaven, breeze, tranquil, peaceful, bliss, Elysian quiet, divine, lasting, silent nature's breathing life. And the landscape is composed in exactly the same way as all the earlier sublime landscapes, with the sea, earth and sky as the basic components in a cosmic geometry.

It is this universal unity that falls apart in the poem.

Such, in the fond illusion of my heart,
Such Picture would I at that time have made:
(...)

So once it would have been, – 'tis no more;
I have submitted to a new control:
A power is gone, which nothing can restore;
A deep distress hath humanised my Soul.
(stanzas 8-9)

The lines doubtless refer to the effects of his brother's death, but their meaning goes beyond that. For despite the brother's death having been the result of a chance happening, Wordsworth's reaction is not. It is in logical continuation of the movement away from the poetical outlook which had already been under way for a long time, and which the brother's death merely accentuated. Although Wordsworth completed *The Prelude*, 1805, in the middle of May, that is to say after his brother's death, the hope heard in the very last line of the poem: "Not without hope we suffer and we mourn" (verse 15), cannot be interpreted as the hope of a return to the view of the imagination and the Sublime that the mirror image originally represented. Our examination of *The Prelude* has shown that.

A kind of poetical revolution thus takes place around the hoary old castle – "thou hoary Pile". It is not possible to maintain the picture of the castle reflected in the smiling sea as a valid expression of how the poet sees nature and himself.

> Not for a moment could I now behold
> A smiling sea, and be what I have been:
> (stanza 10)

This transformation can be measured in a specific vital sphere: in the idea of light that is fundamental to all the early writings, and which is first seriously questioned in *Intimations*. The words in stanza 4 on the poetic freedom to see the world – like the child – in a different light: "add the gleam/The light that never was", compress Wordsworth's poetical practice from an earlier period. We first meet it – in fact in a questioning form – as far back as the old boat poem in the bard's sweet and necessary dream. This questioning is absent in *Descriptive Sketches*, 1793, where in one of the earliest examples of a sublime landscape description in his oeuvre Wordsworth portrays the sun's appearance – "the fire-clad eagle's wheeling form" – during a storm in the Alps.

I have chosen to quote the entire passage and – in the notes Wordsworth's later comment on it – in order to establish two things: firstly that Wordsworth perfectly well and at an early stage knew the sublime tradition which he later transcended; and secondly that his defence of the artistic treatment of the impression corresponds to his view of the inner eye, the light coming from within, which imagination throws on the world in 1798-1800:

> Wide o'er the Alps a hundred streams unfold,
> At once turn'd that flame with gold;
> Behind his sail the peasant strives to shun,
> The west that burns like one dilated sun,
> Where in a mighty crucible expire
> The mountains, glowing hot, like coals of fire.
> (PW I p.62 ll.342-347)

From the picturesque landscape grow its sublime dimensions.[93]

The six lines from *Descriptive Sketches* point the way forward to Wordsworth's view of the impression and his use of light 1798-1800. A couple of examples must suffice. An essential twofold example is the lines so often quoted from *The Prelude*, 1799, "... and make our infancy a visible scene/On which the sun is shining" and the idea of "the auxiliary light" that throws its light even on the sun, likewise from *The Prelude*. Mention could also be made of the passage from *Home at Grassmere:* "yet unto me I feel/That an internal brightness is vouchsafed/That must not die, that must not pass away./Why does this inward lustre fondly seek/And gladly blend with outward fellowship?"

It is this sovereign, glorious inner light, the disappearance of which is the subject of *Intimations*. Instead of the individual, self-illuminating poet's eye, this poem plants a divine, protective eye of light in the firmament. Not even such compensation seems possible any longer in *Elegiac Stanzas*, where this distant, divine light has vanished too. The words from stanza 4 on the light that never was, now take on a quite new significance. From meaning the light which the inner eye casts on the world, so that its true dimensions become visible, "The light that never was" now with retrospective force comes to mean quite literally what the words say: the light that has never existed because it is an illusion. Remaining in *Elegiac Stanzas* are only the flashes of lightning in the deluge-torn scenery in Beaumont's picture: "the lightning, the fierce wind, and trampling waves" (stanza 14).

Here, the fundamental sublime elements emerge again: light, breeze and the reflecting water, but in a broken, dismissive form. The path of meditative contemplation, of cosmic reflection towards the Sublime has been definitively blocked. But at the same time a remarkable transformation takes place in the poem, which can be seen as an artistic move to take the consequences of the collapse of the mirror structure. Where the castle has so far been portrayed as a pile of stones, a grey cliff, that is to say at one with grand nature, the sea in which it was reflected, it is now changed to a man-made creation in the midst of a sea that no longer is merely vibrating, but in violent turmoil and for that very reason cannot reflect. It is this sea, this nature, that has destroyed the poet's brother – and his belief in the reconciling force of the imagination. Instead, like a man-made structure, the poem tries to defy nature: The castle is no longer a

rough stone pile ("rugged", "hoary"), but a gigantic, sublime *human* construction, a "Castle".

> And this huge Castle, standing here sublime,
> I love to see the look with which it braves.
> Cased in the unfeeling armour of old time,
> The lightning, the fierce wind, and trampling waves.
> (13)

While from before 1798 and until 1804 the poem for Wordsworth
reflected a cosmic order, now it has to establish an order within itself. The
Sublime is no longer to be found in the correspondence between nature
and the mind, but in man's heroic defiance of nature: "welcome fortitude,
and patient cheer" (stanza 14); "Not without hope we suffer and we
mourn" (stanza 15). It is a kindred defiance that finds expression in the
obvious distance adopted to physical nature in *Snowdon* and *Simplon* in
the upward movement of imaginative power and spiritual love; and which
at the same time in *Elegiac Stanzas* finds its symbolic expression in the
storm-ridden, immovable castle in Beaumont's painting – as anti-nature,
sublime art.

APPENDIX

Wordsworth reflected in Turner

Wordsworth and Turner were involved in essentially the same project of exploring the Sublime in Man and Nature. They both set out from the well established eighteenth century view of the Sublime as can be gathered from Wordsworth's *Descriptive Sketches* and Turner's treatment of sublime subjects in paintings like *The Shipwreck*, 1805, and *The Passage of the St. Gothard*, c.1804. But in their involvement with the dialectical correspondence of nature and mind, they were to take a radical turn away from the conventional treatment of the Sublime, each in his own way. Thus, what Wordsworth accomplished in a short span of months in 1798-1799 – and abandoned a few years later – was to be a life long ambition on Turner's part carrying his art far beyond the borders of tradition. The prospects of *Norham Castle* by Turner on the front and back cover of this book – and the mirrored landscape from *Lake Llanberris with Dolbadern Castle* c. 1799 inside it – are only faint suggestions of this very complex process.

The process could be summed up by comparing the two versions of *Norham Castle* from respectively 1798 and c. 1840-45. In the older one the sun is reflected in physical, created nature: water and cliffs, in the younger the earthly world itself is penetrated by light, the light or the sun being an omnipresent part of matter.

The first one marks Turner's familiarity with and indebtedness to the old metaphysical tradition of the liber naturae, according to which the divine sun reflects itself in earthly nature – here on the cliffs and in the water – very much like the Arndt-illustration shows. Now, what happens in the development of Turner's work is, that the world as consisting of distinctive phenomena is dissolved into light. That is light presenting itself to the active human eye as colour in the interaction of light and darkness. In this process the two suns – the heavenly and the reflected one – become one. This can be seen if one compares in the *Regulus*, 1828, completed in 1837 with *Dido building Cathage, or the Rise of the Carthagian Empire*, 1815. In the latter Turner is not only involved in a boasting match with Claude Lorrain (*Seaport with the Embarkation of the Queen of Sheba*, 1648). He is also, just like Claude, subscribing to the notion of the divine sun reflecting itself in earthly nature. In the light of this sun all human enterprises take place. People and societies, even the mightiest, perish. The sun, however, endures. In *Regulus* Turner tells the story (from Horace) about Regulus being blinded by the Carthagians who cut off his eyelids exposing his eyes to the blazing sunlight. This all-pervading, sublime – both life-giving and destructive light – is the true object of Turner's ambition. From his contemporaries we know that the light emanating from the canvas seemed so shockingly strong that people could not bear to look at it.

This amazing painting heralds Turner's later works in the 1840'ies (especially from Venice and Lake Geneva) in which the horisontal line separating heaven from its spiritual reflection in earth or water is dissolved or at least blurred. By doubling light in reflection and simultaneously erasing the separating horisontal line Turner created an image of total light or colour. *Sun Setting over a Lake*, c.1840, can serve as an example of this breathtaking destruction of the old mirror of nature.

The two suns becoming one does not, however, result in the total disappearance of the horisontal line as a means of composition consequently abandoning the mirror function. The cow in the Norham Castle-painting from 1840-45 is actually mirorred, but the appearance and significance of these elements of structure change radically. In this respect one could truly speak of one sun and a new kind of sun. From being a reflection of a reflection, i.e. an indirect mediation of the true, eternal light – the *lux intelligibilis* which cannot be percived through the human senses – the mirror-reflection now takes on a new impact. Instead of upholding a clear distinction and a one-way, *vertical* line of communication between the divine and the human, the function of mirroring now consists in creating a *horisontal* correspondence between the sensing subject and the sensed object. The eyes of the perceiving subject are no longer situated within a vertical pattern of seing, but are directed inwards at the depths created by the blurred horisontal line and the single and obscure source of light. This fundamental reorientation strongly resembles the decisive change in Wordsworth's poetry in 1798-1799.

With the dissolution of the horisontal line heaven and earth are no longer separate pictorial entities. But this change is not exclusively technical. Its implications are ideological in so far as there is no longer need for a reflecting/mirroring object or function mediating between the eye that sees and the sun seen as in the engraving from Trauber's *Nervus*

Opticus or Arndt's *Liber naturae*. In this fundamental redirection of the eyes a new metaphysics and a corresponding phenomenology arises, subsequently to be explored further by other artists in the second half of the century.

Turner, then, does not attempt to depict the sun casting its rays on and being reflected in the landscape as in *Norham Castle*, 1798, or *Llanberis* c.1799. The object of his exploration is no longer nature as *landscape*, but as *light* presenting itself in colour in its eternal dialogue with shade or darkness. Turner's work slowly proceeds from landscapes bathed *in* light to landscapes *of* light. In this daring movement the sharp contours of phenomena including the horisontal line are suspended. Thus the difference between the divine and the human realm is erased. But Turner avoids the immanent danger of solipsism, because to him the human eye is both object and subject. Like Wordsworth he insists that his work is in keeping with universal laws governing the human mind – in Turner's case the laws inherent in the interaction of colour and the eye.

By insistingly attempting to catch the interrelation of eye and light in the shades of colour, the ageing Turner pursued his own stubborn course in exploring the potential of the metaphysical implosion – as can be seen for instance in the version of *Norham Castle* from 1840-45 and in his socalled colour beginnings. Although they have often been given a title these works do not have a well defined subject in the strict sense of the word. They rather seem to be at one with their expression. "Nature" here is no longer a specific entity: a landscape, a sun, a lake, but the very nature activated by the expression of colour in the eye of the beholder. In this way the beholder of the painting confronts himself, his own – not private, but objectively human, cosmic – nature in the painting. Like in a mirror. In *Sun setting over a Lake* from around 1840, the sun literally seems to have become both a cosmic eye and a mirror-reflection of the observing eye of the painter – and consequently of the beholder of the painting.

Notes

1. Bowie, 1990, p.1.

2. Quotation taken and translated by W.Glyn Jones from Jørgen Dehs's article *Subjektet og begyndelsen* in Hans Hauge (ed.) *Subjektets status*, Aarhus 1990, p. 18; ... are from Dehs's text, (...) are my own.

3. Cf. PW I p. 317 Wordsworth's note: "The beautiful image with which this poem concludes, suggested itself to me while I was resting in a boat along with my companions".

4. Cf. later the sister's central role in *Tintern Abbey* and in Book 13 of *The Prelude*, 1805.

5. F.W.J. Schelling, *Ausgewählte Schriften*, Band 1, 1794-1800, Frankfurt am Main 1985, p. 696. As will be seen, Wordsworth both agreed and disagreed with Schelling, whom he apparently did not know in 1798-1799. From 1798 until 1804-1805, the relationship between inner and outer was dialectic, non-hierarchical for Wordsworth. Thus, for him the outer world was not a reflection of man's inner world around 1798-1800. This difference is something which E.D.Hirsch Jr. overlooks in *Wordsworth and Schelling*, New Haven 1960, although his comparison of the two under the overall concept of enthusiasm has much to recommend it.

6. *Ludvig Holbergs Memoirer* (The Memoirs of L.H.) ed. F.J. Billeskov Jansen. Anden reviderede udgave, København 1963, s. 85.

7. Quoted from A. Wilton: *Turner and the Sublime*, Chicago 1980, p. 26

8. Goethe, *Faust*, Basel 1944

9. Epistle to the Romans, 1,20: "For the invisible things of him from the creation of the world are clearly seen, being understood by the things that are made, even his eternal power and Godhead." (King James Version)

10. Translated from quotation in Olaf Pedersen: *Naturens bog - strejftog omkring et metaphor i Naturens bog*, ed. Sv. Andersen, Århus 1986, p. 25.

11. Anders Arrebo: *Ossa Rediviva* 1616-1618. Translated from *Samlede Skrifter*, Copenhagen 1965-1984, Vol. 3, p. 45.

12. Quoted from Ernest Lee Tuveson: *The Imagination as a Means of Grace*, Berkeley and Los Angeles, 1960, p. 71.

13. Quoted from Arvidsson, 1990, p.38.

14. Cf. Jurgis Baltrusaitis *Der Spiegel*, Gießen 1986 (1978). Baltrusaitis argues that the usual interpretation of St. Paul's words about the glass as signifying an imperfect reflection is incorrect. "Die Alten haben ihre Spiegel übrigens nicht für mangelhaft und in ihnen abgebildeten Gestalten verdunkelnd gehalten. Ganz im Gegenteil, man hielt gerade das für ein Symbol der Genauigkeit und Klarheit" p.84. On the contrary the mirror was a means of divination. Thus Baltrusaitis quotes J. Filere (1636): "Wenn der Heilige Paulus (...) sich der beiden Ausdrücke Spiegel und Rätzel bedient, um uns zu verdeutlichen, wie wir in der Dunkelheit dieses Erdenlebens Gott erkennen können (...), dann kann es in diesem Zusammenhang nicht verkehrt sein, euch hier einen Spiegel in einem Rätzel und ein Rätzel in einem Spiegel zu zeigen." p.85. This interpretation of "speculum" is supported by the greek text; cf. for instance *Sprachlicher Schlüssel zum Griechischen Neuen Testament* nach der Ausgabe von D. Eberhard Nestle. Bearb. v. Fritz Rienecker, Gießen-Basel 1966, p. 405: "Das Moment 'wie im Spiegel' hat hier keinesfalls abschwächende Kraft, sondern ist hier das schauende Aufnehmen, und zwar ein adäquates Aufnehmen wie in einem guten Spiegel (...)".

15. Quoted from M.H. Abrams: *Natural Supernaturalism*, New York 1973, p. 101.

16. Quoted from Stephen Jay Gould: *Time's Arrow, Time's Cycle*, London 1987, p. 47.

17. Marjorie Hope Nicholson: *Mountain Gloom and Mountain Glory*, Itacha N.Y. 1959, p.143. Tuveson did not have a chance to read Nicholson's book, which in certain respects expresses the same opinions but far more clearly.

18. Otto himself points to the relationship between the two concepts. "Zuerst: auch das 'Erhabene' ist, mit Kant zu reden, ein 'unauswickelbarer Begriff'. (...) Dazu kommt zweitens dass auch am Erhabenen jenes eigentümliche Doppelmoment eines zunächst abdrängenden und gleichzeitig doch wieder ungemein anziehenden Eindruckes auf das Gemüt ist. Es demütigt und erhebt zugleich (...)". At the same time Otto emphasises that "Religiöse Gefühle sind nicht ästhetische". *Das Heilige*, München 1979, p.56ff.

19. ibid. p.24.

20. ibid. p.42.

21. Lars Christiansen: *Naturfilosofi*, København 1980, p.35.

22.. Ann Bermingham: *Landscape and Ideology. The English Rustic Tradition 1740-1860*, Berkeley and Los Angeles 1988, pp.13-14.

23. Quoted from *The Spectator*, No. 477, Saturday, 6 September, 1712.

24. C.C.L. Hirschfeld: *Theorie der Gartenkunst,* Hildesheim – New York 1973, Vol. I, p. 163 (Leipzig 1779-1780).

25. According to PW II, Wordsworth himself dated the poem to 1799. I have chosen to follow Jonathan Wordsworth's dating in *The Borders of Vision*, p.31.

26. Wordsworth uses the idea of the positive aspect of the Sublime in largely the same way as Burke.

27. The texts alternate between first and third person as does the first version of *There was a boy* indicating perhaps that Wordsworth is closing in on, but not yet clearly decided upon, what was soon to be a deliberate autobiographical project.

28. The text has been adjusted to coincide with Jonathan Wordsworth's redaction in *The Borders of Vision*, p.379ff.

29. Cf. *Home at Grasmere*, 1800, PW V p.328 ll.427-470, in which Wordsworth writes about the simple, but noble feelings that are the foundation of any society: "They lift the animal being, do themselves/ By Nature's kind and ever-present aid/ Refine the selfishness from which they spring,/ Redeem by love the individual sense/ Of anxiousness with which they are combined". (ll.454-458) Here it becomes clear that this purification encompasses the moral aspect of man and – in continuation of this – that Wordsworth like Kant and Schiller considers the elevated mind as *morally* elevated.

30. Compare the fragment with *The Prelude*, 1799: "The mind of man is fashioned and built up/Even as a strain of music". (N p.492 ll.1-2) and *The Prelude*, 1799 (N p.3 ll.67-68).

31. Cf. *The Prelude*, 1805 V l.619.

32.. These characteristics are to be found again in the *Simplon* poem.

33. If we read *Tintern Abbey* biographically, the earlier poet is a young man who has emerged from puberty, while the boy in *The Ruined Cottage* and later in *The Prelude*, 1799 (apart from the last section in Part Two) is in the main aged less than nine. It is a striking and repeated characteristic of Wordsworth that he does not seem to be concerned with reliability and

consistency in the relationship between age and psychology in contrasting the spontaneous and the reflective relationships to nature.

34. In the last part of the poem Wordsworth speaks in praise of his sister, in her unspoiled relationship to nature recognising his own original one: "in thy voice I catch/The language of my former heart, and read/My former pleasures in the shooting lights/Of thy wild eyes". (PW II p.262 ll.116-119) From these eyes he glimpses the life that has been lost: "these gleams/Of past existence". (PW II p.263 ll.148-149)

35. This view is supported by the fact that in many important respects Wordsworth transfers the respective order of the fragments to the finished text, and that the further we progress, the more philosophical the poem as a whole becomes. Thus the crucial new formulations in relation to the fragments occur in the last third of the first part of the poem.

36. It is not my intention to deny that the river - in line with so many other natural phenomena in Wordsworth - has what from the point of view of literary analysis must be called a symbolical function, but on the other hand to argue that this symbolical function must be considered in the light of Wordsworth's view on the relationship between nature and consciousness.

37. The section is heralded in *The Ruined Cottage*, where the boy's mind is formed in a relationship with nature that is not free from fear: "communion not from terror free" (PW V p.381 l.78)

38. In his dissertation of *The Sublime and the Beautiful* from 1811, Wordsworth discusses the Sublime and the child's experience of it in a distant and theoretical tone which not only echoes Burke and Kant, but also shows how far he was in 1811 from the position he adopted in 1798-1799. After noting that sublime objects lose their power when one becomes intimate with them, he turns to the child's attitude: "Yet it cannot be doubted that a Child or an unpractised person whose mind is possessed by the sight of a lofty precipice, with its attire of hanging rocks & starting trees &c., has been visited by a sense of sublimity, if personal fear & surprize or wonder have not been carried beyond certain bounds". (PrW II p.353 ll.136-140) Compare also to the previous quotation of Gray on his mountain experience.

39. In fact, this also stands in first place in the *JJ* manuscript and can therefore reasonably be considered Wordsworth's initial attempt to examine the relationship between consciousness and nature, as he had described it in *Tintern Abbey*.

40. I have considered this subject in *Himmelstormerne*, Copenhagen 1993, (*The Titans*) unfortunately only available in Danish.

41. In relation to the fragment there are some major changes which are mainly due to the fact that in 1799 Wordsworth expanded some lines about the winter's games in the two above-mentioned, independent episodes; in addition there are some minor changes, the most important of which is that "spirits" in 1799 is replaced by "genii".

42. There is here a repetition of the cosmic picture of the sea from the skating expedition. In terms of simple chronology, however, this latter picture is the original one, as it is found in the *JJ* manuscript. This sea - with its double significance as a physical phenomenon and the source of human emotion - corresponds to "beatings of the heart". And it is related to the analogy between the great spirits and the vibrating surface of the water in the 1794 fragment. See also the analysis of *There was a boy* p.95ff.

43. l. 50. In *The Prelude*, 1799, the word has been changed to "intertwine".

44. Cf. The *Preface* to the second edition of *Lyrical Ballads*, 1800: "as acting and re-acting upon each other" (PrW I p. 395).

45. This is the process Wordsworth seeks to describe in the passage considered above from *The Ruined Cottage*, ll. 70-94.

46. Wordsworth's metaphor of drink and spring stems presumably from the association with the suckling child, but fits in at the same time with the water metaphor.

47. This section uses the same concepts for the sublime as Burke.

48. Cf. *Preface* to *Lyrical Ballads*, 1800, PrW I pp.86-88.

49. Cf. the final line of *There was a boy*.

50. The dream state and meditative preoccupation appear to be closely related. Cf. for instance *The Ruined Cottage* PW V p.381 l.94 and fragments *iv* and *v* in the *Alfoxden* notebook, and also the *Christabel* manuscript fragment *ii*.

51. Cf. the occasions when Wordsworth speaks of drinking from nature: l,395: "drinking in a pure organic pleasure" and 2,360: "did I drink the visionary power".

52. We meet this idea again in the *Ode: Intimations of Mortality*, 1802-1804, but here it is developed into an entire theory on pre-existence and birth as an irreparable fall.

53. The criticism is presumably aimed at 18th-century mechanism. Cf. M.H.Abrams: *The Mirror and the Lamp*, Oxford (1953) 1971, p.67.

54. Within the compass of Wordsworth's own literary and intellectual horizon, this tradition is most strongly represented by Milton and Blake.

55. Cf. the Danish author M.A.Goldschmidt's novel *Arvingen* (The Heir), 1865, which in the introduction addresses the function of memory on the basis of similar considerations: "I thought it was easy to tell where you were born, and how your childhood passed; but in trying to look back in memory and if possible seize the first thing I can remember, I realise how fruitless it would be to attempt a task that forces its way upon me: to unroll that strangely enclosed and yet so open and receptive life in which is formed an interwoven series of images, states and impressions that create the background to our entire later life, is the source of many subsequent thoughts, sympathies and antipathies, of our longings, and indeed of outbursts of will and energy". A similar significance as a source of moral values is ascribed to childhood by Wordsworth, cf. the end of *The Prelude*, 1799, Part Two ll. 465-496.

56. Some scholars have questioned the biographical interpretation of this particular passage – with biographical arguments; the biographical factor however is not crucial to my reading, which is rather concerned with the boy's inevitable, biologically and psychologically determined move towards independence, resulting in his separation from maternal ties.

57. Cf. Wordsworth's later comment (from 1814) on the problem of immortality in *Intimations* (PW IV p.464): "The poem rests entirely upon two recollections of childhood, one that of away, and the other an indisposition to bend to the law of death as applying to our particular case. A reader who has not a vivid recollection of these feelings having existed in his life cannot understand that poem."

58. The 1798 version:
          "There was a boy – ye knew him well, ye rocks
And islands of Winander, and ye green
Peninsulas of Esthwaite – many a time
[   ] when the stars began

To move along the edges of the hills,
Rising or setting, would he stand alone
Beneath the trees or by the glimmering lakes,
And through his fingers woven in one close knot
Blow mimic hootings to the silent owls,
And bid them answer him. And they would shout
Across the wat'ry vale, and shout again,
Responsive to my call, with tremulous sobs
And long halloos, and screams, and echoes loud,
Redoubled and redoubled – and a wild scene
Of mirth and jocund din. And when it chanced
That pauses of deep silence mocked my skill,
Then often in that silence, while I hung
Listening, a sudden shock of mild surprize
Would carry far into my heart the voice
Of mountain torrents; or the visible scene
Would enter unawares into my mind
With all its solemn imagery, its rocks,
Its woods, and that uncertain heaven, received
In the bosom of the steady lake."
(N p.492)

59. See for instance Paul de Man's lecture *Time and History in Wordsworth*, originally given in 1967 and revised in 1971 to include a discussion with Geoffrey Hartman. Published in *Diacritics*, 17:4, 1987. I have discussed de Man's revised paper with reference to *There was a boy* in *Kritik* 112, 1994, pp. 6-16.

60. Cf. *The Prelude*, 1799: "that vainglory of superior skill", N p.15, l.69.

61. This is a process closely related to the sinking into the mind which Wordsworth describes in the passage discussed earlier: "The calm water lay upon my mind" etc.

62. In Weiskel, 1967, Thomas Weiskel has suggested the plausible interpretation of the Sublime that the downwards movement corresponds to introspection, but the movement upwards the transcendental. In Wordsworth's case this distinction does not hold, for the two directional indicators are elements in a superior, dialectical experience of the Sublime.

63. Cf. *The Prelude* and fragment *iv* from the *Christabel* manuscript: "The ear hears not; and yet, I know not how,/More than the other senses does it hold/A manifest communion with the heart" (PW V p.343).

64. Wordsworth argues in a similar way when speaking of the poet's ability to generate feelings, which he defines in this way: "an ability of conjuring up in himself passions, which are indeed far from being the same as those produced by real events". (PW II p.393).

65. I am aware that it is possible to find inconsistencies of both a theoretical, philosophical and logical kind in the programmatic foreword. It is thus not without reason that in *The Anatomy of Criticism* Northrop Frye refuses to give Wordsworth, the top poet in the class, more than a B plus as a theorist: "Wordsworth's Preface to *Lyrical Ballads* is a remarkable document, but as a piece of Wordsworthian criticism nobody would give it more than about a B plus." (Quoted from the Atheneum edition, 1968, p.5). I prefer Wordsworth the poet to Wordsworth the theorist – if he ever was one.

66. I have based my analysis on Jonathan Wordsworth's dating and textual criticism in *The Borders of Vision*, p. 390.

67. Cf. N p.497 ll.50-52: "A large unmutilated rainbow stood/Immovable in heaven [?] [?been] [?]/ With stride colossal bridging the whole vale." Draft for the Five-Book Prelude, February 1804.

68. p.187

69. *The Prelude*, 1799. N p.16 ll.115-116

70. Cf. *Tintern Abbey* "whose dwelling is the light of setting suns" and the whole of the fundamental image in the poems from 1787 and 1789.

71. Cf. M.H. Abrams, 1973, p. 74. Abrams also includes the Kûnstlerroman.

72. McConnell, 1974, p.2.

73. I refer to the chapter entitled *Den verdslige naturmetafysik* in Klaus P. Mortensen: *Himmel-stormerne*, 1993.

74. This and the previous dating are taken from the critical notes to the text in the Norton edition.

75. The passage is not found in the manuscript to Book Fourth from 1804, the first part of which is spoiled and therefore only begins in what now in 1805 is line 270, but it may well date back to March 1804.

76. Compare this with the end of Book Twelfth: "an ennobling interchange/Of action from within and from without:/The excellence, pure spirit, and best power,/Both of the object seen, and the eye that sees".

77. This stage is not portrayed just once and for all, but is a recurring theme from Book Third right through to Book Twelfth.

78. With various changes of stance, especially in the case of the passage on "spots of time", revised formulations and excisions, Books First and Second in 1805 correspond to *The Prelude*, 1799.

79. It is presumably this to which he is alluding when, writing on the delight gripping the reader in the encounter with "great Nature" found in the works of great poets, Wordsworth comments: "visionary power attends the motions of the winds/embodied in the mystery of words". (N p.184 ll.619-621). Here, in crystalline form, Wordsworth describes the possibility of experiencing the Sublime which poetry offers. Cf. later Wordsworth's explicit dream of writing a sublime work which emerges towards the end of *The Prelude* (written early in 1805), and which he envisions as a natural force. (N p.452 l.309)

80. Here Wordsworth might be alluding to – and at the same time pessimistcally inverting – the impact of Ch. 13,12 in *The First Epistle of Paul the Apostle to the Corinthians*: "For now we see through a glass, darkly; but then face to face: now I know in part; but then I shall know even as also I am known".

81. It must always be remembered that, even less than in 1799, *The Prelude* 1804 and 1805 consists of unambiguous texts, not least because, although they were thoroughly rewritten, they contain strata from various phases in Wordsworth's writings in the form of passages incorporated without alteration. As will be seen later, this applies for instance to the 1805 Book Seventh, ll.722-730, which hark right back to a fragment dated January-February 1798.

82. The earliest version of this passage contains a section that was later incorporated into Book Eighth, ll.711-727. Here, the disappointment is compared with the traveller who enters a cave

and by the light of torches experiences a variety of living forms in the play of the light in the darkness. But this impression of the new world gradually congeals, until it lies before his eyes: "lifeless as a written book". Things are not that bad in 1805, when the inanimate is given life. (N p.304 ll.711-727).

83. Cf., in order: 1799 1,1; 1,26; all 1799 and 1805, especially Books First and Second; 1805 9,1-9; 1799 2, 247-249; 1805 13, 172: "the stream".

84. Similar expressions of Wordsworth's old faith in the dialectic between physical nature and the human mind can be found in the draft material from the Five-Book *Prelude* from February – early March 1804. In a passage leading up to the description of Snowdon Wordsworth elaborates on the correspondence. Higher minds can trace the "analogy betwixt/ The mind of man and Nature" (N p.497 ll.27-28). Similarly, in a draft for Book Eighth from October 1804 he speaks of the growing boy, reflecting upon himself: "He feels that be his mind however great/ In aspiration, the universe in which/ He lives is equal to his mind, that each/ Is worthy of the other – if one/ Be insatiate, the other is inexhaustible./ Whatever dignity there be [ ]/ Within himself from which he gathers hope,/ There doth he feel its counterpart, the same/ In kind before him outwardly expressed,/ With diffrence that makes the likeness clear,/ Sublimity, grave beauty, excellence/ Not taken upon trust, but self-displayed/ Before his proper senses;" (N p.504 ll.170-182).

85. The biography dates it to 1791. Wordsworth's first description of this experience, which contains many points of similarity with *The Prelude* is found in *Descriptive Sketches*, which was written in 1792 (cf. Jonathan Wordsworth *The Borders of Vision*, p.311-312). The following passage can be seen as an attempt at picturesque landscape portrayal and its conception of the Sublime is, according to J. Wordsworth, strongly inspired by Beattie's *The Minstrel*, 1771. "– 'Tis morn: with gold the verdant mountain glows,/ More high, the snowy peaks with hues of rose/ Far stretch'd beneath the many-tinted hills,/ A mighty waste of mist the valley fills,/ A solemn sea! whose vales and mountains round/ Stand motionless, to awful silence bound./ A gulf of gloomy blue, that opens wide/ And bottomless, divides the midway tide./ Like leaning masts of stranded ships appear/ The pines that near the coast their summits rear/ Of cabins, woods, and lawns a pleasant shore/ Bounds calm and clear the chaos still and hoar:/ Loud thro' that midway gulf ascending sound/ Unnumber'd streams with hollow road profound./ Mounts thro' the nearer mist the chant of birds,/ And talking voices, and the low of herds,/ The bark of dogs, the drowsy tinkling bell,/ And wild-wood mountain lutes of saddest swell./ Think not, suspended from the cliff on high/ He looks below with undelighted eye." (PW I p.72 ll.492-511).

86. Cf. the significance of the waters in *There was a boy*.

87. Cf. for instance, also: "the lesson of love" (PW V p.382 l.116) and: "in their silent faces did he read/Unutterable love" (PW V p.382 ll.127-128) as examples of this anthropomorphisation of nature and naturisation of the human.

88. N p. 489 ll.109-114.

89. Cf. the interpretation of *Simplon*.

90. Cf. the two earlier images of thawing frost in which first the breeze and then the soul are the force creating spring.

91. A loss that is repeated in the death of Wordsworth's brother John in February 1805.

92. Sometimes the dates are other than those suggested by the reminiscing poet's chronology.

93. Wordsworth himself made the following comment on his description in a note to the 1793 manuscript (A). I quote it in extenso because it points forward to the position taken in 1798-1799 on the imagination and its relation to grand nature: "I had once given to these sketches the title of Picturesque; but the Alps are insulted in applying to them that term. Whoever, in attempting to describe their sublime features, should confine himself to the cold rules of painting would give his reader but a very imperfect idea of those emotions which they have the irresistible power to communicate to the most impassive imaginations. The fact is, that controuling influence, which distinguishes the Alps from all other scenery, is derived from images which disdain the pencil. Had I wished to make a picture of this scene I had thrown much less light into it. But I consulted nature and my feelings. The ideas excited by the stormy sunset I am here describing owed their sublimity to that deluge of light, or rather of fire, in which nature had wrapped the immense forms around me; any intrusion of shade, by destroying the unity of the impression, had necessarily diminished its grandeur." (PW I p.62 note) This contest with painting here ends to the advantage of poetry. Poetry is more capable of conveying the impression, that is to say the feelings or ideas which the grandiose Alpine landscape creates or awakes in the beholder: the sublimity in the torrent of light or fire in the storm-surrounded sunset awakens a sublimity in the poet, the impression forms the mind. A significant correspondence arises here between what is sensed and the person sensing, the phenomenal exterior and the emotional interior nature – "nature and my feelings" – to which the poet is artistically bound. Only by consulting nature and his own inner reaction to the impression of it can he retain and convey the unity with which the supreme cosmic light robes the world – in the original impression. In other words, artistic truth arises in the dialectic between reception and creation.

Literature

M. H. Abrams: "English Romanticism: The Spirit of the Age" in: Bloom, 1970

M. H. Abrams: *Natural Supernaturalism. Tradition and Revolution in Romantic Literature*, New York 1973 (1971)

M. H. Abrams: *The Mirror and the Lamp*, London, Oxford, New York 1971 (1953)

M. H. Abrams (ed.): *Wordsworth. A collection of Critical Essays*, Englewood Cliffs 1972

Joseph Addison: *Addison and Steele. Selections from the Tatler and the Spectator.* (Introd. and notes by Robert J. Allen), New York 1970

Svend Andersen (red.): *Naturens bog*, Århus 1986

Anders Arrebo: *Samlede Skrifter*, København 1965-1984

Bengt Arvidsson: Naturlig teologi och naturteologi. Naturen som bild i dansk fromhetstradition omkring år 1600, *Studia Theologica Lundensia* 45, Lund 1990

Irving Babbitt: *Rousseau and Romanticism*, Austin and London, 1977

Jeffrey Baker: *Time and Mind i Wordsworth's Poetry*, Detroit 1980

Jurgis Baltrusaitis: *Der Spiegel*, Gießen 1986 (1978)

John Barrell: *The Idea of Landscape and the Sense of Place 1730-1840*, Cambridge 1972

Joseph Warren Beach: *The Concept of Nature in Nineteenth-Century English Poetry*, New York 1936

Ernst Behler og Jochen Hörisch (Hrsg.): *Die Aktualität der Frühromantik*, Paderborn et al. 1987

Poul Behrendt: *Viljens former*, København 1974

Lise Bek (red.): *Naturopfattelse og landskabsæstetik*, Århus 1989

Peter L. Berger: *The Social Reality of Religion*, Harmondsworth 1973 (1967 with the title *The Sacred Canopy*)

Ann Bermingham: *Landscape and Ideology. The English Rustic Tradition 1740-1860*, Berkeley, Los Angeles, and London 1988

Alfred Biese: *Das Naturgefühl im Wandel der Zeiten*, Leipzig 1926

Jonathan Bishop: "Wordsworth and the 'Spots of Time'" in: Harvey et al. 1972

Harold Bloom (ed.): *Romanticism and Consciousness*, New York 1970

Michael Bockemühl: *Turner*, Køln 1993

Karl Heinz Bohrer: *Die Kritik der Romantik*, Frankf. a.M. 1989

Hans Boll-Johansen og Fl. Lundgreen-Nielsen (red.): *Kaos og kosmos*, København 1989

Andrew Bowie: *Aesthetics and Subjectivity*, Manchester and New York 1990

Thomas Bredsdorff: *Digternes natur. En idés historie i 1700-tallets danske poesi*, København 1975

Thomas Bredsdorff: "Lovejovianism – Or the Ideological Mechanism", *Orbis Litterarum*, vol. 30, København 1975

Peter Bricknell: *Beauty, Horror and Immensity. Picturesque Landscape in Britain 1750-1850*, Cambridge 1981

Cleanth Brooks: *Poetisk struktur*, København 1968, trans. of *The Well Wrought Urn*, 1947

196

Stig Brøgger, Else Marie Bukdahl og Hein Heinsen: *Omkring det sublime*, København 1987 (1985).

Edmund Burke: *A Philosophical Enquiry into the Origin of our Ideas of the Sublime and Beautiful* (ed. and introd. by Adam Phillips), Oxford, New York 1990 (1757)

David Carr: *Time, Narrative, and History*, Bloomington/Indianapolis 1991 (1986)

Cynthia Chase (ed.): *Romanticism*, Singapore 1993

Lars Christiansen: *Naturfilosofi*, København 1980

Kenneth Clark: *Landscape into Art*, New York 1979 (1949)

R. G. Collingwood: *The Idea of History*, Oxford 1978 (1946)

R. G. Collingwood: *The Idea of Nature*, Oxford 1965 (1945)

Paul Crowther: *The Kantian Sublime. From Morality to Art*, New York 1991 (1989)

Ernst Robert Curtius: *Die Ideallandschaft* in: *Europäische Litteratur und lateinisches Mittelalter*, Bern 1948

Helen Darbishire: "Wordsworth's *Prelude*", in: Harvey et al. 1972

Jørgen Dehs: "Subjektet og begyndelsen" in: H. Hauge (red.): *Subjektets status*, Århus 1990

Jørgen Dehs (red.): *Æstetiske teorier*, Odense 1984

Matthias Eberle: *Individuum und Landschaft. Zur Entstehung und Entwicklung der Landschaftsmalerei*, Giessen 1986 (1979)

Henning Eichberg & Ejgil Jespersen: *De grønne bølger. Træk af natur- og friluftslivets historie*, Slagelse 1986

T. S. Eliot: *The Use of Poetry and the Use of Criticism*, London 1964 (1933)

Christian Elling: *Den romantiske Have*, København 1942

William Empson: "Sense in *The Prelude* " in: Norton 1979

Manfred Frank: *Die Unhintergehbarkeit von Individualität*, Frankf. a.M., 1986

Northrop Frye: *Anatomy of Criticism*, New York 1965 (1957)

Max J. Friedländer: *Landskapet och andra motiv i måleriet*, (trans. of *Essays über die Landschaftsmalerei und andere Bildgattungen*), Stockholm 1951

Clarence J. Glacken: *Traces on the Rhodian Shore*, Berkeley and Los Angeles, 1967

Hans-Georg Gadamer: "Frühromantik, Hermeneutik, Dekonstruktivismus", in: Behler et al. 1987

Hans-Georg Gadamer: *Wahrheit und Methode*, Tübingen 1975 (1960)

Rodolphe Gasché: *The Tain of the Mirror*, Cambr. Mass., and London 1986

Ronald Gaskell: *Wordsworth's Poem of the Mind*, Edinburgh 1991

Johann Wolfgang Goethe: *Faust*, Basel 1944

Stephen Jay Gould: Time's Arrow, Time's Cycle. *Myth and Metaphor in the Discovery of Geological Time*, London 1987

Stipe Grgas og Sv. E. Larsen (eds.): *The Construction of Nature*, Odense 1994

Götz Grossklaus og Ernst Oldemeyer (eds.): *Natur als Gegenwelt. Beiträge zur Kulturgeschichte der Natur*, Karlsruhe 1983

Christa Hackenesch (ed.): *"Bin so ausgeworfen aus dem Garten der Natur". Texte und Bilder zur Geschichte einer Sehnsucht*, Hamburg 1984

Geoffey H. Hartman: "Romanticism and 'Anti-Self-Consciousness'" in: Bloom 1970 and Chase 1993

Geoffrey H. Hartman: *Wordsworth's Poetry 1787-1814*, Cambridge, Mass. and London 1987 (1964)

W. J. Harvey and R. Gravil (eds.): *Wordsworth's The Prelude. A Casebook*, London and Basingstoke 1972

Justus Hartnack: *Fra Kant til Hegel. En nytolkning*, København 1979

Jørgen Hass: "Verdens-anskuelse – romantikken og filosofien" in: *Kritik* 83

James A. W. Heffernan: *The Re-creation of Landscape*, Hannover and London 1984

James A. W. Heffernan: *Wordsworth's Theory of Poetry. The Transforming Imagination*, Itacha and London 1969

Aage Henriksen, Erik A. Nielsen og Knud Wentzel: *Ideologihistorie I. Organisme-tænkningen i dansk litteratur*, København 1975

Neil Hertz: "The Notion of Blockage in the Literature of the Sublime" in: Chase 1993

Walter John Hipple: *The Beautiful, The Sublime, and The Picturesque in Eighteenth-Century British Aestetic Theory*, Carbondale Ill. 1957

Christian C. L. Hirschfeld: *Theorie der Gartenkunst*, Hildesheim-New York 1973 (Leipzig 1779-1780)

E. D. Hirsch Jr.: *Wordsworth and Schelling*, New Haven 1960

Jens-Jørn Holmen: *Fra landskab til livsverden. En metafysikkritik*, Århus 1986

Jens-Jørn Holmen: "Landskab. Fra natur som rum til natur som tid" in: Lise Bek (red.), 1989

John Dixon Hunt: *The Figure in the Landsacape: Poetry, Painting, and Gardening during the Eighteenth Century*, Baltimore og London 1976

Mary Jacobus: "Splitting the Race of Man in Twain" in: Chase 1993

Alun R. Jones and W. Tydeman (eds.): *Wordsworth Lyrical Ballads. A Casebook*, 1972

John Jones: *The Egotistical Sublime*, London 1954

Immanuel Kant: *Kritik der Urteilskraft* (Werkausg. bd. X von Wilhelm Wieschedel), Wiesbaden 1990 (1790)

Paul Kluckhohn: *Das Ideengut der deutschen Romantik*, Tübingen 1953

Karl Kroeber and W. Walling (eds.): *Images of Romanticism*, New Haven and London 1978

Ulla Britt Lagerroth och Margareta Ramsay: *Romantiken över gränser*, Lund 1993

Robert Langbaum: "The Evolution of Soul in Wordsworth's Poetry" in: Harvey et al. 1972

Robert Langbaum: *The Mysteries of Identity. A Theme in Modern Literature*, Chicago and London 1982 (1977)

Herbert Lehmann: "Die Physiognomie der Landschaft" in: *Studium Generale* Jg. 3 Heft 4/5 April 1950

Herbert Lindenberger: "Images of Interaction in *The Prelude*" in: Norton 1979

"Longinos": *Den store stil*, transl. and introduction by Niels Møller, København 1934

Arthur O. Lovejoy: *The Great Chain of Being. A Study of the History of an Idea*, Cambridge, Mass. and London 1976 (1936)

Lennart Lundmark: *Tidens gång och tidens värde*, Södertälje 1989

Roland Lysell: "Det romantiske landskab" in: *Det ny Poetik* nr. 2

Heinrich Lützeler: "Vom Wesen der Landschaftsmalerei" in: *Studium Generale* Jg. 3 Heft 4/5 April 1950

Aage Lærke: "Edens haver. Tekst og billeder" in: *Kritik* 50

K. E. Løgstrup: *Kants æstetik*, København 1964

J. R. MacGillivray: "The Three Forms of *The Prelude*" in: Harvey et al. 1972

Paul de Man: "Intentional Structure of the Romantic Image" in: Bloom, 1970

Paul de Man: "Time and History in Wordsworth" in: Chase 1993

Odo Marquard: "Kant und die Wende zur Ästhetik" in: *Zeitschrift für philosophische Forschung* XVI/2 og 3, 1962

Odo Marquard: *Tranzendentaler Idealismus Romantische Naturphilosophie Psychoanalyse*, Köln 1987

Frank D.McConnell: *The Confessional Imagination*, Baltimore and London, 1974

Winfried Menninghaus: *Unendliche Verdopplung*, Frankf. a. M. 1987

H. E. Mittig: "Funktionen des Landschaftsbildes" in: *Kritische Berichte* 2. Jg. 1974 Heft 3/4

Samuel H. Monk: *The Sublime. A Study of Critical Theories in XVIII-Century England*, New York 1935

Mary Moorman (ed.): *Journals of Dorothy Wordsworth*, London, Oxford, New York 1976 (1958)

Mary Moorman: *William Wordsworth: A Biography. The Early Years 1770-1803*, Oxford 1968 (1965)

Mary Moorman: *William Wordsworth: A Biography. The Later Years 1803-1850*, Oxford 1969 (1957)

Klaus P. Mortensen: *Himmelstormerne. En linje i dansk naturdigtning*, København 1993

Klaus P. Mortensen: "Det sublimes natur" in: *Kredsen* 61. årg. nr. 1, 1995

Klaus P. Mortensen: "Spejlinger" in: *Kritik* 127

Klaus P. Mortensen: "That false secondary power. Natur og bevidsthed hos Wordsworth – og de Man" in: *Kritik* 112

Lis Møller: "Erindringens Poetik. William Wordsworth og psykoanalysen" in: *Kritik* 83

Lis Møller: "Landskabets tid" in: *Det ny Poetik*, nr. 2

Marjorie Hope Nicolson: *Mountain Gloom and Mountain Glory. The Devopment of the Aestethics of the Infinite*, Itacha, N.Y. 1959

Erik A. Nielsen: *Søvnløshed*, Århus 1982

Richard J. Onorato: "*The Prelude*: Metaphors of Beginning and Where They Lead" in: Norton 1979

Rudolph Otto: *Das Heilige. Über das Irrationale in der Idee des Göttlichen und sein Verhältnis zum Rationalen*, München 1979 (1917)

Frederick A. Pottle: "The Eye and the Object in the Poetry of Wordsworth" in: Bloom 1970

Graham Reynolds: *Turner*, London, 1992 (1969)

F. W. J. Schelling: *Ausgewählte Schriften* Band 1 1794-1800, Frankf. a. M. 1985

Friedrich Schiller: *Sämtliche Werke* Bd.V, München 1968

Friedrich Schiller: *Werke und Briefe* bd. 8, Frankf. a.M. 1988

Paul D. Sheats: *The Making of Wordsworth's Poetry, 1785-1798*, Cambr. Mass. 1973

Martin Schwind: "Sinn und Ausdruck der Landschaft" in: *Studium Generale* Jg. 3 Heft 4/5 April 1950

Erich Steingräber: *Zweitausend Jahre Europäische Landschaftsmalerei*, München 1985

Frederik Stjernfelt: Interview med Jean-François Lyotard in: *Information* 22.6. 1992

Frederik Stjernfelt: *Rationalitetens himmel og andre essays*, København 1997

L. J. Swingle: "Wordsworth's "Picture of the Mind" in: Kroeber et al. 1978

C. Th. Sørensen: *Europas havekunst*, København 1959

Ernest Lee Tuveson: *The Imagination as a Means of Grace*, Berkeley and Los Angeles 1960

Poul Erik Tøjner: *Poetik - at tænke med kunst*, København 1989

J. R. Watson: *Picturesque Landscape and English Romantic Poetry*, 1970

Rolf Wedewer: *Landschaftsmalerei zwischen Traum und Wirklichkeit*, Köln 1978

Thomas Weiskel: *The Romantic Sublime: Studies in the Structure and Psychology of Transcendence*, Baltimore 1976

Knud Wentzel: "Personlighedsudvikling" in: *Ideologihistorie* I, København 1975

Basil Willey: *The Eighteenth Century Background. Studies on the Idea of Nature in the Thought of the Period*, London 1974 (1940)

Andrew Wilton: *Turner and the Sublime*, Chicago 1980

A. O. Wlecke: *Wordsworth and the Sublime*, Berkeley, L.A. and London 1973

Jonathan Wordsworth: *William Wordsworth. The Borders of Vision*, Oxford 1982

Keld Zeruneith: "Dannelsesromanens metode", in: *Kritik* 38